Beacon

of

Hope

Catalyst for Change: Building a Better World

Table of Contents

Find us on Facebook @KellyMarkeyAuthor, Instagram @Author_Kelly_Markey and LinkedIn @kellymarkey

Paperback ISBN: 978-1-7636837-5-4

Cover Design: Markey Writing Academy
Layout: Markey Writing Academy
Typesetting: Markey Writing Academy

Markey Writing Academy
Central Coast New South Wales,
Australia 2250
www.kellymarkey.com

A Change Maker's Pledge

For those who dare to rise, lead, and transform the world.

I am a Change Maker.
I am called to ignite transformation within my sphere of inţuence.
I know my Creator,understand my identity, and walk boldly in my divine purpose.
I am a steward of hope, a vessel of leadership, and a representative of heaven on earth.

My presence here is intentional. My time is a sacred assignment.
I rise with conviction to lead with integrity and take dominion in my calling.
I seek Ţrst the principles of peace, equity, and justice for all humanity.
I work not for personal gain, but to uplift, restore, and reform broken systems.
I labour not just to provide for my household, but to build a legacy for generations.
I am not driven by proŢt, but by purpose.

My life is a testimony of action, compassion, and unwavering truth.
I pursue impact, create income with integrity, and steward inţuence for the greater good.
I live to inspire change and embody hope in motion.
I am a Change Maker.

Governance is not the exclusive duty of politicians -
It is the sacred responsibility of every awakened soul.
True leadership begins with self-mastery: the governance of one's thoughts, actions, and values.

Only then can we rise to govern communities, organisations, and nations.
Nation-building is not a solo act. It is a collective mission.
Each of us has a role.
Each of us carries the power to change the world

Agape,
Kelly Markey

Praise for the Book

Beacon of Hope: A Catalyst for Change is a global game-changer—a powerful anthology curated by bestselling, award-winning author Kelly Markey, shining with the soul of humanity. Published by Markey Writing Academy, this holy grail of hope unites voices from around the world to inspire real social change.
CBS News

In *Beacon of Hope: A Catalyst for Change*, Kelly Markey delivers a soul-stirring manifesto that transcends borders, race, and circumstance. This is not just a book—it's a movement. Through gripping personal stories, global narratives, and a deep well of compassion, Markey lights a fire in the reader's heart to believe in the power of one voice, one act, and one moment to create lasting change.

What sets this book apart is not only Markey's powerful vision but also the extraordinary chorus of co-authors who bring their lived experiences to life with raw honesty and resilient hope. Each contributor adds a unique lens—survivors, change-makers, warriors, and dreamers—who weave a tapestry of transformation together. Their stories are not merely anecdotes; they are beacons in their own right, reminding us that courage is contagious and collective healing is possible.

This book is both a mirror and a call to action. It reflects the brokenness in our world while daring us to become part of the healing. Markey's voice is tender yet unflinching—equal parts visionary and warrior. With poetic precision and a prophetic tone, she challenges readers to live with purpose and to be the hope they are searching for.

Beacon of Hope is more than a read, it's a revolution in print, a must-have for anyone seeking meaning, impact and inspiration in uncertain times.
The Post

A global call to action—Beacon of Hope is the lighthouse in the storm.
ABC News

Curated by Kelly Markey, *Beacon of Hope* is a powerful global anthem for hope and change.
NBC News

Beacon of Hope: A Catalyst for Change is a powerful book emphasising the importance of living with empathy and compassion, prioritising society's and humanity's well-being over personal gain. It urges readers to remain constantly aware of how their actions and inactions can impact their communities and the wider world.
Melvin Tarlue, journalist and media relations management expert

Foreword

Listening and acknowledging another person's experience should never be minimised. Creating a space for someone to be seen, heard, and acknowledged is the most important gift we can provide to another.

My friend and I were waiting for the other members of our high school youth group to arrive. We stood side by side, staring out the window and looking towards the park down the street. My friend suddenly announced matter-of-factly, "My mother moved us (her siblings) to my grandmother's house. My parents are getting divorced." She proceeded to share the events that led to the event. She reported the information without vocal inflections or pauses. I glanced at her and continued to look out of the window. She had provided cold, hard facts, but I knew that she was in pain. When she paused, I acknowledged how hard this change must be.

A few minutes later, I shared my home life and that we had more in common than we realised. We had a chance to share our truths. I experienced a sense of relief when I found out that I was not alone. While our family wouldn't change for the better anytime soon, being seen and heard made it bearable. I was not the only one experiencing family challenges. I was not alone. We spoke for a few minutes and then looked out the window quietly until it was time for the meeting to begin.

When you read Kelly's and my bios, you may think that I am an unlikely choice to write this foreword. Kelly lives in Australia, and I live in the Greater New York area.

Kelly has devoted her life to science and is a respected thought leader and award-winning author who speaks about spirituality, leadership, and business.

On the other hand, I have a background in Human Resources and carved out a space using humour and storytelling to champion the importance of human connection. I have been known to "complain" in my New York way about my fellow humans' struggles to "see each other" and communicate meaningfully.

Before meeting Kelly, I had spent the prior decade finding my creative voice and stepping out of my comfort zone. Adding humour and narrative storytelling to my toolkit has allowed me to finally let myself be seen and heard authentically, delivering keynotes, workshops, and humorous stories in public.

However, the world is smaller than we think, and it affords us amazing opportunities to connect and learn from others with different backgrounds, if we pay attention and take the chance to connect. And so, it was with Kelly and me. We met at a writer's group on Zoom a few years ago. She was working on an endless list of manuscripts in the making. I was in the process of the second edition of my humorous *"The Learned-it in Queens Communications Playbook – Winning Against Digital Distraction."* I added a witty workbook section (aka homework!) that my readers could use to improve their communications and get out of their way.

What drew me to Kelly was her honesty and her sense of purpose. Like me, she believed in using the power of authentic stories to disrupt how people see themselves and others. While I was using humour to cajole others into a laughing state of self-awareness, Kelly used personal stories of tragedy while navigating and trying to make sense of her experiences.

Now, while it may appear we were approaching life as complete opposites, this was not the case. We both believe that healing self-awareness starts with accepting our truths and appreciating the big and small moments that shaped our humanity. Both of us grew up in a world where you hide your pain and pretend things didn't happen or that it didn't matter. But at a certain point in our lives, we responded to that approach with the question, "Who does this serve?" As a result, we began to mine for personal stories and share them in a profoundly personal way.

When Kelly Markey decided to launch into the world of self-publishing the following year and launch the publication, *"Echoes of Humanity, Exploring Human Wonders Through the Pages of: Lessons, Affliction, Triumph, Victory and Brilliance,"*

Kelly was able to organise an incredible tribe of contributors in a stunningly short amount of time. While most of us were writing an outline, she already had a business plan, contributors, and a production schedule in place.

She accomplished this because of her incredible team (which includes her supportive and incredibly multi-talented husband and champion Dave Markey), and because her authors trusted her implicitly. Kelly had led by example through her writings. When she courageously shared her truths, she created a space allowing others to do the same. We don't choose our families or circumstances. Many of us grew up in homes that required us to assume a family narrative that called for us to behave in specific ways that would protect a premise, an image, or a secret. In "Beacon of Hope Anthology," the writers invite us into their lives as they share inspiring, compelling, and at times tragic stories.

This book is not an anthology built on perfect, curated AI-generated prose, but with raw stories packed with lessons. These writers display great courage as they relay tales of domestic and sexual abuse, violence, and crime. The authors bring light to behavioural and mental health challenges and traumatic, life-changing experiences.

The book also touches on topics that do not receive the attention they deserve. The topics include arranged marriages, a foster child's experience, the painful realities of widowhood, and more.

These are raw, authentic narratives written in the inner voices the authors have held in their hearts for years. Their feelings of fear, sadness, and depression didn't heed the call for perfect phrasing and punctuation. Doing so would have caused them to lose the essence of these authors' struggles to claim and share. To expect conformity would have prompted these authors to reconsider committing their words to paper and impeded their sharing.

As a result, these authors bare their souls, not to feed their ego but to serve others. They shared these stories for you and me.

They've taken their pain and converted it into their purpose. The writers understand that their experiences don't represent isolated incidents. They represent countless others across the globe. This knowledge gave them the courage to share. Verushka Solomon writes, "I'm sharing my story not to complain about my childhood, but for you to stay hopeful and believe in yourself. Ask for help if you need it. Go for counselling, it is nothing to be ashamed of."

What the writers' narratives embody is a key component in storytelling—context. They shared their "Why?" wrapped in sensory elements, emotions, and painful facts. The result is that the authors created memorable stories that yield countless, compelling lessons. Personal narratives are recognised as a powerful healing tool, but the writers don't merely leave the readers with a heartfelt tale to contemplate. They share what made a difference in their ability to move from one state of being to another. Their faith, teacher's or life partner's kindness, and inner resilience were acknowledged.

In addition, they've created a "playbook" for others to follow and shared the resources they found or created to support those in similar circumstances. This sense of hope is what makes this anthology important and inspiring. Their message is clear from Patricia to Seema and all the other contributors. "We are not alone. We raised our voices and allowed ourselves to be seen so others will do the same."

I close this foreword with a heartfelt acknowledgement to an amazing group of writers who are using these pages to encourage you to find the courage to make the changes you've been struggling to make.

Julienne B. Ryan
Communications Catalyst
J. Ryan Partners – Be engaged

Publisher's Preface

Shining a Light on Social Change: Dynamics, Catalysts, and Implications

Social change transforms a society's beliefs, behaviours, attitudes, and structures over time. It can occur through various mechanisms such as cultural evolution, technological advancement, political movements, economic shifts, and changes in social norms. Social change can be gradual or sudden, intentional or unplanned, often resulting from complex interactions among individuals, groups, and institutions within a society.

Social change is a phenomenon that has intrigued scholars and researchers across disciplines for decades. It encompasses transforming societal beliefs, behaviours, norms, and structures over time, reflecting the evolving dynamics of human interactions and institutional frameworks. This article explores the multifaceted nature of social change, examining its drivers, mechanisms, and profound implications for individuals, communities, and societies.

Drivers of Social Change

Various factors, including cultural evolution, technological advancements, economic developments, political movements, and shifts in social norms, propel social change. These drivers influence different societal aspects, contributing to gradual and abrupt transformations.

Cultural Evolution: Changes in cultural values, beliefs, and practices over generations shape societal norms and behaviours. This evolution is often influenced by communication, media, education, and global interconnectedness, leading to the adoption of new ideas and discarding outdated practices.

Technological Advancements: The rapid pace of technological innovation accelerates social change by altering how individuals interact, communicate, work, and access information. Technologies like the internet, social media, and artificial intelligence have revolutionised social dynamics and organisational structures.

Economic Developments: Economic forces play a pivotal role in social change by influencing employment patterns, wealth distribution, consumption habits, and living standards. Economic crises, globalisation, and shifts in market demands can catalyse societal restructuring and adaptation.

Political Movements: Social movements, revolutions, and political ideologies advocate for change in governance, policies, and social justice. They mobilise collective action, challenge existing power structures, and promote inclusivity, equality, and human rights.

Shifts in Social Norms: Changing attitudes towards gender roles, family structures, sexuality, and diversity reflect evolving societal values and expectations. Generational differences, education, advocacy, and awareness campaigns often drive these shifts.

Mechanisms of Social Change

Social change manifests through diverse mechanisms that shape the trajectory and outcomes of transformation within societies:

Institutional Change: Reformations in legal frameworks, governance structures, and organisational practices facilitate societal adaptation to new challenges and opportunities.

Cultural Diffusion: The spread of ideas, behaviours, and practices across geographical and cultural boundaries influences societal norms and customs.

Collective Action: Social movements, protests, advocacy campaigns, and grassroots initiatives mobilise individuals to challenge injustices, demand reforms, and promote social equality.

Technological Disruption: Innovations disrupt existing industries, create new economic opportunities, and redefine social interactions and communication patterns.

Implications of Social Change

The consequences of social change are profound and wide-ranging, impacting individuals, communities, institutions, and global systems.

Individuals and Communities: Social change shapes identities, aspirations, lifestyles, and opportunities for personal growth and fulfilment. It fosters diversity, inclusivity, and empowerment while challenging stereotypes and social inequalities.

Institutions and Organisations: To remain relevant and sustainable, organisations must adapt to changing societal expectations, regulatory environments, and technological advancements.

Global Dynamics: Social change transcends national borders, influencing global interconnectedness, geopolitical relations, and collective responses to global challenges such as climate change, pandemics, and migration.

Becoming a Catalyst for Change: Changing the Global Narrative Through Personal Experience

In the tapestry of history, social change often arises from the intersection of individual courage and collective action. Throughout time, movements have flourished when ordinary people decided to step out of the margins and challenge the status quo, using their personal experiences as the driving force for a broader societal shift. Today, we find ourselves at a pivotal moment in the world's evolution, where the power of individual narratives, fuelled by lived experiences, can transform local communities and the global landscape.

To be a catalyst for change is to recognise the vast, yet often untapped, potential within one's own experiences and perspectives. Each person's life story is filled with lessons learned, struggles overcome, and insights gained—all valuable resources for making a meaningful difference.

As society becomes increasingly interconnected, the call to

contribute to social change has never been louder or more urgent. The global challenges we face today—whether environmental degradation, racial inequality, discrimination, hikes in suicide and human welfare issues, or economic injustice—demand a new kind of leadership. This leadership is not always rooted in traditional power structures but in the courage of individuals who dare to share their stories and advocate for a better, more inclusive world.

The Power of Personal Narratives

At the heart of social change lies the concept of narrative. Every society is built on stories that shape values, inform policies, and guide behaviours. Historically, many of these narratives have been told by the powerful and the privileged, often marginalising the voices of those who have been oppressed or silenced. However, as the world becomes more inclusive and diverse, the role of personal narratives has taken centre stage. When individuals speak from their experiences, they bring forth a raw, authentic, and often transformative truth.

The significance of personal stories in the context of social change cannot be overstated. Narratives of struggle, resilience, and survival can humanise complex issues, making them accessible and relatable to a broader audience. Take, for example, the Civil Rights Movement in the United States, where individuals like Rosa Parks and Martin Luther King Jr. used their personal experiences with racism and injustice to fuel a larger movement that challenged systemic discrimination. Similarly, figures like Malala Yousafzai have shared their individual journeys of adversity in the fight for girls' education, sparking global dialogue and action on the issue.

What makes these stories so powerful is their authenticity? They come not from abstract theories or statistics but from lived experience. They act when people hear first-hand accounts of hardship, resilience, and victory. These stories resonate emotionally, bridging the gap between individuals who may never have experienced such struggles but can empathise with the human need for dignity, fairness, and equality. By telling these narratives, social change takes root, grows, and ultimately transforms the world.

Global Connectivity and Collective Action

The rise of global connectivity has exponentially amplified the power of personal stories. Social media platforms, blogs, and online forums have created spaces where voices that once went unheard can now be amplified. The digital age has enabled people from every corner of the world to share their experiences, connect with like-minded individuals, and build communities of support that transcend geographical boundaries.

This interconnectedness presents a unique opportunity for collective action on a global scale. Social movements today are often global, with individuals from diverse backgrounds coming together around shared causes. Movements like #MeToo, Black Lives Matter, and Fridays for Future have gained momentum because people can share their experiences and stand in solidarity with others who face similar struggles, regardless of where they live. The ability to connect and organise across borders has created a more cohesive global movement for social justice.

However, this also means that the responsibility for creating social change is no longer limited to a select few. Regardless of their background or position, every individual has the potential to influence the global conversation. When brought together, the collective power of personal stories and experiences can catalyse monumental shifts in how societies view and address issues such as inequality, injustice, and human rights.

Leveraging Lived Experience for Change

While the power of personal narratives is undeniable, it is not enough to share one's story. To truly be a catalyst for social change, individuals must intentionally leverage their experiences. The question then becomes: How can one use their life experience to create a lasting impact?

The first step is to recognise the inherent value of one's own story. Many people, especially those from marginalised communities, may feel their experiences are insignificant or not worth sharing. However, precisely these experiences have the power to shed light on issues that often go unnoticed. Whether it's a story of growing up in poverty, facing discrimination, or struggling with mental health, each narrative carries the potential to spark empathy and action. By telling these stories, we can begin to reshape the global narrative.

Once individuals recognise the power of their stories, the next step is to find platforms to share them, which can be done through social media, blogs, podcasts, or public speaking events. By making their voices heard, individuals can inspire others to act, while drawing attention to critical issues that need urgent attention.

Furthermore, becoming a catalyst for change requires a commitment to continuous learning and advocacy. Sharing one's story is only the beginning. Actual change comes from the willingness to engage in ongoing dialogue, to listen to others, and to work collaboratively toward solutions. Individuals committed to social change must also be open to evolving their perspectives, as the world is constantly changing, and so must our strategies for addressing its challenges.

The Role of Empathy and Solidarity

In the pursuit of social change, empathy and solidarity are crucial components. As more individuals step forward to share their personal experiences, others must listen with open hearts and minds. Empathy allows individuals to connect with the experiences of others, even if they have not lived them themselves. It fosters understanding and compassion necessary for building a more just and equitable world.

Solidarity, on the other hand, goes beyond empathy—it is the active commitment to standing with others in their struggle for justice. This means using one's platform, privilege, and resources to support those fighting for change. Whether advocating for policy changes, raising awareness about critical issues, or providing financial or emotional support to grassroots organisations, solidarity strengthens social movements and amplifies their impact.

Empathy and solidarity are passive and active forces that propel social change. When individuals stand together in pursuit of a common goal, their collective efforts are far more potent than the sum of their individual actions.

The Ripple Effect of Personal Transformation

One of the most profound aspects of becoming a catalyst for change is the ripple effect that personal transformation can have. When one uses their life experience to challenge the status quo, they create a chain reaction that can impact countless others. This is the essence of social change: the idea that one person's actions can inspire others to take up the cause, creating a growing movement.

Consider the example of climate activism. Greta Thunberg, a young Swedish activist, began her journey by striking from school to protest climate change outside the Swedish parliament. What started as a solitary act of defiance quickly turned into a global movement that has inspired millions of young people worldwide to demand action on climate change. Thunberg's experience witnessing the environmental degradation in her country and the lack of political action catalysed a global conversation about the planet's future.

The ripple effect extends beyond the individual. When people witness someone else stepping forward with their story and acting, they are often inspired to do the same. This creates a culture of activism and change, where individuals recognise their power and responsibility to shape the world around them.

Building a Global Mission

At its core, social change is about reimagining our world and creating a new narrative that is more inclusive, just, and equitable for all. This requires the collective effort of individuals, communities, and organisations working together toward shared goals. The narratives of those who have lived through hardship and injustice must be at the forefront of this movement, guiding the way for a more compassionate and fair future.

Becoming a catalyst for change is not a solitary endeavour. It is a shared responsibility that calls upon everyone to use life experiences as a tool for transformation. The more individuals are willing to step forward, share their stories, and advocate for change, the more likely the global narrative will shift toward greater justice and equity.

Social change is a dynamic process driven by cultural, technological, economic, political, and social factors. It shapes the fabric of societies, fostering innovation, progress, and resilience while confronting challenges of inequality, injustice, and resistance to change. Understanding the complexities of social change is essential for policymakers, leaders, and individuals to navigate and harness its transformative potential for creating inclusive, equitable, and sustainable futures.

During another trip to the USA in 2024, I had the profound opportunity to visit Washington, DC, where I explored many iconic landmarks; however, two sites touched me profoundly. They are both deeply connected to Dr Martin Luther King Jr. My journey began at the Martin Luther King Jr. Memorial, where I reflected on his powerful words about hope. The experience was profoundly moving, especially considering his famous quote: *"We must accept finite disappointment, but never lose infinite hope. Out of the mountain of despair, a stone of HOPE."*

Martin Luther King Junior Memorial in Washington DC

I encountered profound moments of introspection, encounters that set my spirit ablaze with renewed purpose. At the Martin Luther King Jr. Memorial, I stood before the mighty "*stone of hope*," carved defiantly from a "*mountain of despair.*" It was not just a sculpture but a living metaphor, a reminder that hope can rise from the rubble of heartbreak and injustice, unshakable and magnificent. Dr King's words, *"We must accept finite disappointment, but never lose infinite hope,"* pulsed through me like a lifeline, bridging past and present, sorrow and possibility.

Later, as I climbed the steps of the Lincoln Memorial, I stood where Dr King once stood, delivering his dream to the world on August 28, 1963. The date rang deep within me. August 28 is also the day I was born. It was as though time had folded in, linking my personal journey to a greater, timeless dream, a call to be more, to *become* a living embodiment of **HOPE**.

In those sacred spaces, I realised that the *Beacon of Hope* is not just an idea. It is a revolution of spirit. It is a call to every heart to rise, to dream fiercely, and to act boldly. It is the steady flame passed hand-to-hand across generations, lighting up the dark corners of despair, injustice, and fear. It felt like a profound alignment of my journey with Dr King›s vision.

Reflecting on these experiences, I realised how my mission, the Beacon of Hope, aligns closely with Dr King's legacy. The mission seeks to change the global social narrative and transform dreams into tangible realities. It's more than just a dream. It's a purpose-driven reality that feels deeply connected to the principles Dr King championed.

Being at both the memorial and the Lincoln Memorial, feeling that alignment, was a powerful reminder of the ongoing relevance of Dr King's vision and the impact of our collective efforts to foster hope and change. It was an honour to walk in his footsteps and be inspired by his enduring legacy.

What legacy are you creating? How are you impacting humanity? What are you aligned to? The power of social change lies in the ability of individuals to harness their lived experiences and use them as catalysts for a better world. Every story, no matter how small or seemingly insignificant, has the potential to make a difference.

In an increasingly interconnected world, each person's voice matters. By becoming a catalyst for change and working together in solidarity, we can rewrite the global narrative and create a more just, equitable, and compassionate world for future generations.

Kelly Markey
Founder and CEO of Markey Writing Academy and Beacon of Hope Mission
International Bestselling and Award-winning Author
Global and Award-winning Publisher
Featured on the New York Times Square Billboard

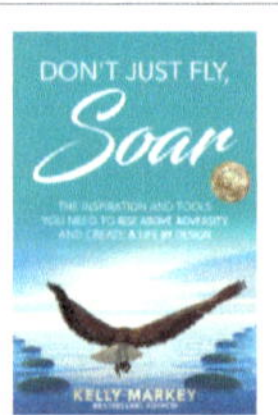

If you are looking to advance your business or personal portfolio:
Make Sage Decisions, Advocate for Social Justice, Ambassador of Hope, Craft Resilience, Suicide Awareness and Navigate Discrimination, **I am your Maven!**
Author, Speaker, Change Maker, Business Pundit, Facilitator, Subject Matter Expert, Corporate Coach and Publisher

Introduction

In a world often dimmed by despair, *Beacon of Hope* rises like a lighthouse amidst a storm-tossed sea, its light piercing through darkness, guiding the lost, and steadying the shaken. This mission is not just a ripple in still waters but a tidal wave of compassion, crashing against the shores of indifference. Like a tree whose roots dig deep into purpose and whose branches stretch toward humanity, it bears fruit that feeds souls, not egos.

The legacy we build through selfless action does not fade like footprints in the sand but etches itself into the bedrock of eternity. Through love, justice, and mercy, what we carve into the lives of others transcends time, echoing in the hearts of generations to come. What we do for ourselves may be buried with our bones, but what we do for others becomes immortal, like a constellation blazing forever in the night sky.

As the founder of the global Beacon of Hope Mission, I am compelled to create anthologies that shine a light on lived experiences so we can make a better world. Motivation is like morning mist, pretty, poetic, and gone by noon. We do not need another sugar-coated TED Talk or a quote wrapped in gold foil. The world needs fire at our feet, a clock ticking loud in our ears, and a reason so fierce it makes stagnation unbearable.

Most people do not need more inspiration—they need more consequences.

We are floating in a sea of "*you got this*" posts, trying to build ships out of good vibes. Meanwhile, the winds of time keep blowing, and we stay anchored in the harbour—safe, still, stuck. Deadlines are missed. Dreams gather dust. Marketing plans? Abandoned.
Big visions? Shrinking. Why? Because staying the same does not come with a fine. No one is billing you for wasted potential.

However, here's the truth:

You are not stuck because you do not have goals. You are stuck because comfort is your captor, and it refuses to scream, but instead it soothes. No one is certainly coming to haul you out of your rut. This is your rescue mission. Newsflash! Change does not arrive like a sunrise. It crashes like a storm when you finally get sick of your excuses and refuse to waste one more day playing small. If you are waiting for clarity, stop. Forge it like steel through heat and pressure. If you are waiting for courage, forget it. Walk forward, scared. And perfection? That's a myth sold to keep you polishing instead of progressing.

If you genuinely want to be a catalyst for global change, raise the stakes. Set the cost of inaction so high you cannot afford to sit still. The world does not need another comfort-seeker. It needs bold builders, relentless starters, and truth-tellers who cannot be bought by convenience. You hold the spark. You are the matchstick. The wildfire of **HOPE** begins with your decision to strike. The only thing in your way is you. Now move!

There are moments when destiny feels tangible, like standing at the intersection of history and purpose, with its breath pressing gently against your skin, whispering," You *are part of this."* My visit to the Smithsonian Museum in Washington, D.C., was one such moment. As I stood before the radiant Hope Diamond, its brilliance seemed to pulse with more than just beauty. It held the weight of resilience, legacy, and unshakable promise.

Nearby, a timeless watch ticked in silent rhythm, echoing the urgency of now. These symbols stirred something deep within me, reigniting my mission as the founder of Beacon of Hope: to be a light in a world that too often dwells in shadows. As the diamond is forged under pressure and the watch measures every second, our global mission demands courage, clarity, and action. I invite you, reader, dreamer, change-maker, to come aboard. Let us be catalysts for sustained transformation, igniting hope where it flickers and building a humanity where it flourishes.

Hope Diamond, Symposium Museum in Washington DC

Beacon of Hope: A Catalyst for Change is a living anthology of voices from across the world, each voice a spark, each story a flame, together igniting a bonfire of change that cannot be ignored.

HOPE is not passive. It is not naive.
HOPE is the hammer that shatters despair.
HOPE is the bridge that carries us over the chasms of fear.
HOPE is the anthem that turns dreams into movements and miracles.

As you turn these pages, you are not just reading stories but stepping into a revolution of heart and soul.

What revolution are you igniting?
What dream is waiting for your courage?
What legacy are you daring to leave behind?

The world is not changed by those who stand still.
The world is changed by those who dare to shine.
Be the beacon.

Beacon of Hope stands as a catalyst for global change, igniting a mission rooted in intentional integrity—the very virtue humanity is so intensely thirsty for. In a world fragmented by fear, division, and broken promises, this book serves as a luminous call back to wholeness, reminding us that true transformation begins within. It challenges individuals and communities alike to rise with authenticity, compassion, and unwavering ethical commitment, inspiring a new era where our actions reflect the highest truths of who we are. Through its message, *Beacon of Hope* becomes more than a book; it becomes a living, breathing mission of HOPE, healing, and unity.

There are those who create and those who tear down. Some build bridges with words, hands, and vision, inviting others to cross into places of hope, healing, and possibility. Others burn those bridges with criticism, envy, or fear, tearing down what they never dared to build. Creators understand the cost of construction: the sleepless nights, the silent battles, the persistence to dream in a world that often rewards conformity. They birth ideas, communities, art, movements, and healing.

Destroyers often operate from the shadows, throwing stones at glass houses they have never dared to enter. Their mission? To diminish what they do not understand or cannot control.

The truth:
It is always easier to destroy than to create.
And yet—**only one of those paths leaves a legacy.**

So, choose to be a creator.
Even if your voice trembles.
Even if your hands are tired.
Even if your heart has known deep wounds.

Create anyway.
Because this world needs more builders.
More light bearers.
More voices that dare to say, *"I will rise, and I will help others rise too."*

In a world where success is often measured by titles, possessions, and relentless productivity, I felt a deep call to redefine what it truly means to live a meaningful life. *Beacon of Hope: Catalyst for Change* was born out of this conviction—the belief that success should not consume us but **elevate** us. It should give us room to breathe, reflect, and most importantly, **give back**. Real success enhances our lives and allows us to serve others, not just ourselves. This book is my offering to the world—a reminder that hope is not a vague idea, but a powerful force that, when lived out intentionally, can reshape communities and transform lives.

I did not write this book alone. I invited other co-authors—leaders, survivors, dreamers, poets, artists, and change-makers—so they could shine their light. Together, we have created a collective voice that speaks into the world's brokenness with courage, compassion, and action. *Beacon of Hope* is more than a book. It's a mission. A call to rise, give, and be the light for others. Our hope is not passive—it's **tangible**, lived, and boldly shared for the sake of humanity.

Kelly Markey km

Grace Beyond Shame, HOPE Rising from Brokenness

Introduction

Confronting **Shame** and **Pain**

The pain seems unbearable, feeling confused with anxiety, fear, numb, stuck, and incomplete, with nothing to desire. I felt like an empty road. When we come into this world for the first time, we are all just that empty road. Without understanding words, we are free from any troubles and shame. There was such a beautiful sight in front of me, a lovely view. In the distance, I could see the sun setting; the sky looked breathtaking, making me stop to notice it.

But my heart kept beating faster due to agitation and fear, and I set out on a journey on an empty road, with no idea where it would take me. I continued walking. Through this journey, I came across a pretty butterfly that flew past my face, with tears rolling down my cheeks. As I got closer to home, this empty feeling manifested in confusion about what had happened.

Growing up in a predominantly coloured community and in a family that was loved, or I thought that was family values, my father being the head of the home, and my mother was the homemaker, we lived in a two-bedroom home with six sisters and two brothers. My father was a churchgoer and was seen as a respected elder; whatever happened inside the house stayed in the home. My whole perception of life changed after I was coerced into an unhealthy relationship.

At 16, I found myself pregnant and faced the fear of the unfamiliar. Being a naïve young girl not knowing the ramifications ahead of me, I did not understand what was happening inside my body. There was a massive change within me. I did not have the confidence to tell my mother or my siblings. I had to live with that shame and guilt. I became aloof towards my parents and siblings. Even though I did not tell them, eventually it became known. I had to live with that shame and pain. Living with a heavy burden, I could not express myself freely.

My mom was afraid to let my father know of the situation because my dad played a prominent role in the church, which would embarrass him. I was put into an intense state of emotional stress and turmoil. Due to this fact, I was chased out of the house after my dad got to hear about my pregnancy. After several days, I was allowed to come back home. It brought shame and disgrace to my parents and siblings.

The whispered gossip about their unkind words and judgmental behaviour started amongst family, friends, and neighbours. It says in Leviticus 19:16, "Do not spread slanderous gossip among your people, and you shall not stand up against the life of your neighbour." The silent stares and remarks caused stress and anxiety, and the heavy burden of feeling like a disgrace made me feel like a failure to trust God when confronted with my pregnancy. Yet I was desperately seeking God's Grace. I blamed myself for something that was not my fault. In Romans 3:23, God forgives us for our sins and shortcomings, including when we fail. God gives His gracious forgiveness and the Holy Spirit to those who believe and repent of breaking God's laws. I desperately wanted comfort from God or anyone.

The painful tension at home with my dad, in shock and disappointment, was riddled with guilt. His responsibility over the situation and his prominent role in the church always loomed over me. It was made clear by my dad that the father of my child would be held responsible for child support and expenses, which can be overwhelming at a young age. Anxiety and stress associated with teenage motherhood can have long-term effects on mental health. They can be a challenging experience that affects emotional well-being, social relationships, financial stability, and educational opportunities. It is essential to have the support of family, friends, and community resources, which can play a crucial role in helping teenage mothers navigate these challenges.

With my emotional turmoil of stress during my pregnancy, I went into early labour. My baby was born prematurely, with a high risk of health problems, and was hospitalised for three months. The baby could not breathe due to his lungs not being fully developed and had to receive oxygen. My infant had to be cared for in an incubator, fed by a tube, because his suck reflex was not developed. This tube went directly into his tummy, and he had to receive lots of antibiotics to fight off any infections or potential infections. As a young mother, it took a significant toll on my mental health.

While I was grappling in the vortex, my dad was adamant that my child's father must marry me and take on the role of being a responsible father to his child. I was unhappy to get married at a young age; I had no say in this matter. I asked my dad if I could stay with family members, but he disagreed. I was tossed from the frying pan to the fire, and no empathy came my way.

On the eve of the wedding, I was physically abused. I cried to my mother; I did not want to get married. Unfortunately, my mother had no say in the matter either. My wedding, which should have been the most exhilarating day of my life, was filled with tears, and the words at the altar could not come out. Nightmare was an understatement. I felt like running away from this situation and thought it was all just a dream on an empty road, with no destination. I had to take cognisance that I had a choice in this matter. I was robbed of my youth, and the future had no sign of hope.

After the wedding, we stayed with his family in a one-bedroom house. Life became doing daily chores and caring for my child. He worked and provided for our needs, so the constant arguing and fighting started. Then his priorities shifted to staying out late at night, partying, drinking, and smoking with friends. This routine became the norm every weekend for him. I had to be the submissive wife, staying at home with no voice in the matter. Voiceless yet again.

His mom was diagnosed with stomach cancer, which took a huge toll on the family. Her unbearable pain and constant trips to the hospital did not alleviate her suffering, and she succumbed to her death on April 12, 1982.

Two years into the marriage, I became pregnant with my

second child. Life was a bit calm for a while. Then the fights and arguments started again. He started hitting me, which was nothing new. But this time he punched my stomach. Out of fear of losing my greatest blessing, I begged him to stop hitting my stomach. I was in disbelief. Trauma was unleashed in so many untold ways.

We moved away from the community of Wentworth. I did not want the children to be exposed to the kind of living with gangsters, drugs, etc. Life became unbearable, the constant fighting, and darkness enveloped my soul. Every limb ached and was fatigued, and my eyes were tired from crying all night. Sleep vanished, and dreams remained unanswered, walking on a long, weary, empty road, longing for respite, praying for a way out, my faith unwavering, with each struggle, each fight, each loss, each knock back. I am stoic but exhausted. My low self-esteem made me stay. I had struggled with low self-esteem and self-worth within the marriage. I lumbered on with no absolute joy.

As the years progressed, life became unhealthy and unconducive for the children, seeing how their dad treated me daily. I went to work to contribute to this marriage. It was no walk in the park working and still being abused by this person. I used to get locked up in the room to prevent me from going to work. Life was no bed of roses. He felt that my place should be at home, and be a stay-at-home mom. When the kids were grown, I decided to work again to escape from this mental torture—a little sprinkle of respite.

However, the father of my children continued to belittle and mock me in front of them, not knowing any better. They were kids with these memories of their childhood. Their father was a good provider, but not a DAD. I endured for 29 years, not because I did not know the pain, but because I thought love meant enduring it for the sake of my children. I lost pieces of myself in silence, hoping things would change. I believed that loyalty could fix what was broken. But the truth was that loyalty only prolonged suffering and pain. My soul, body, and mind had no solace. Hope had vanished.

I was a protective, loving, and caring mom. My children's father did not give us that opportunity to be around family to bond and build a healthy relationship, community, or support system.

I could not talk about my life, but my colleagues could see my scars and tears. However, this did not deter me from dreaming of becoming somebody one day. I worked hard, and my superiors saw my potential. It gave me a glimmer of hope.

I aimed to find someone to love me and make me feel valuable. I did not realise I could only attract someone who believed what I already thought about myself. I just figured out that calling me names and hitting me were part of the process of love. Besides, from my early childhood, I had seen women beaten by men who said they loved them. Although it was an unhealthy relationship, I was afraid to let go. I was also convinced that no one else would want me. I thought he was my only chance at love. Although the "love" he gave was not always lovely, in my mind, it was painful. Brokenness reigned, and I felt stuck.

Riding the roller coaster abuse cycle yet again made me trauma bond and contributed to my staying and settling for less than I deserved. He was not always abusive. The abuse cycle had periods of calm, followed by buildup and an explosion. It is a cycle that keeps going. Sometimes, he would shower me with small gifts. Those times would also convince me that it could get better. I hoped the period of calm would stay. A buildup of tension always followed the calm. He would slip and call me a name, kick me, and throw me down the stairs, use profanity, or yell angrily.

Soon after, a significant explosion would occur, sometimes resulting in physical abuse. The bad ones were equally bad. The good times served to keep me working hard to try to get back to the good and try to ward off the bad. I did not realise that I was not in control of the abuse. The abuse was a choice he made, and I could do nothing to stop him from being abusive. I could not end something I did not cause.

The constant change of moving homes did not make life comfortable. The whole process of moving was unbearable, and I felt lost in building stability for the children.

It's a new morning, yet the habits are still the same; I try to hide, smiling over the painful shame. It's a new day at work, and the lies continue to be told. Each co-worker sees a bright smile over a heart that has grown so cold. It's a new night for nightmares, another desperate attempt to sleep.

I convinced myself that I would stay for the children. Constant messages of a woman who cannot raise two children echoed in my mind. The stigma of being a single mother is laced with shame and embarrassment. Although single mothers are doing the good, hard work of parenting, society often paints the picture that they are the problem. I was told that no one worth having would ever want a single mother with two kids, so I stayed because I had convinced myself that being in a bad relationship was better than being single.

I stayed because, in my mind, I had convinced myself that starting over would be hard. Then I found myself there for nearly three decades. People sometimes celebrate a relationship's longevity without questioning the long-term relationship's health. I had made an enormous investment in that relationship. I had worked hard to try to keep it all together. It crushed my soul that I would be walking away from the years of effort I had put in. I feared starting over, not knowing what might be on the other side. I feared what it would be like to be single.

I stayed because I knew that leaving would be dangerous. I feared that I would not live to enjoy the freedom of being free. My abuser had threatened me many times about what he could and would take from me if I left, among his threats that he would "kill" me. The history of violence in the relationship also scared me. He was stronger than I, and I feared he would end my life if I left. Staying was dangerous, but I feared leaving could be even more dangerous.

Fast forward, my husband worked out most of the time, and home was peaceful with just my children and me, until I found out that he was cheating. This cheating behaviour went on for the duration of our marriage. After years of being abused, emotionally, physically, and mentally, and losing our home, I decided to walk out of this marriage with just the clothes on my back. Although I am not sure what we had was ever a great thing, he hurt me badly and told me he loved me, when all he did was isolate me, and all he did was break me down. Everyone told me to walk away, but I feared losing everything important. I did not care about the material things you showered me with.

"Today is the day I am walking away from it all. The emotional abuse is how I feel, and I will no longer be your victim of your emotional abuse. I know I am a wonderful, kind person, and won't allow you to tell me anything different anymore. I am walking away from the abuse today, and you will never be part of my life again. It's time to break free, to end this loop of denying the abuse. A painful past, not me who should suffer, to send the ungodly to trial."

It's time to put away the smile that hides the scars, the enduring pain. I must rise above, soon, with courage. For the very first time, this was the day that I began to live, to see the light, and discover life outside the trauma.

It's time to trust the process of ultimately healing. I went back to school to finish my matric. It took me two years to complete my night school. After receiving my matric, I went to study Safety Management with a diploma. It was not easy starting afresh; it was a daily struggle going through my emotions, but at the end of the day, just knowing that I now have my piece of sanity and knowing that I am a woman who will fear nothing and gain back my independence and life. I rise above brokenness.

The anger was like a ticking time bomb, knowing of the years of being overlooked, dismissed, hurt, and disrespected. It's the silent sacrifices that go unnoticed, unappreciated. I felt lost, loss of everything familiar, everything that was apparently constant; however, toxic, disabling, and disempowering, the relationship loss was real and awakening. My new reality could not find my feet. I was no longer in an abusive relationship.

However, my experience in the relationship impacted me so profoundly that I did not know where I was before the abusive relationship. And where I was heading without a map of life. Indeed, I no longer felt like I was a person before I got entangled in the traumatic relationship. Allowing myself to think and feel what I am scared or hesitant of will take me to the heart of what I need to work out in myself. It was no walk in the park untangling myself from layers of abuse and finding my voice and myself again.

I had to be kind towards myself, set boundaries to regain my confidence, self-esteem, and self-respect. I had to find and get to know her. She was lost in someone else's ideal world. She had to find herself again and regain her SELF ESTEEM, CONFIDENCE, TRUST, VALUE, and most of all LOVE for herself, for who she is.

My dream was to uplift myself as a strong woman with values, core, and principles. As a child, you learn how to crawl, walk, and talk. I found myself in that child again, to know the true meaning of crawling to forgive myself and my abuser, and to hope that someday my abuser will understand the impact of his actions. Until then, I will continue to rise above and build a life filled with love and self-acceptance.

I healed and learned that how people treat you reflects how they feel about themselves, and what you tolerate, you also encourage them to let a person get comfortable with mistreating you.

The Cycle of Pain: How Shame led to vulnerability

The shame, scars, and lessons learned came together in rolling balls of tears, often met with sarcasm and judgment from society. Unintended pregnancy changes the narrative of one's life, the actions and inactions of my family and friends, as well as society, in response to the news of the pregnancy. One is inevitably wrapped with a web of moral judgment by society, family, and friends through subjective perceptions, beliefs, and attitudes, most times without seeking to understand the course of the actions that led to the pregnancy, with all sorts of derogatory names thrown at them. These forms of stigma emanate from various social sources, such as family, school, churches, etc. To avoid or minimise criticism and feelings of guilt and shame, I intentionally isolate myself from family and friends. It lowers one's self-esteem, affects my ability to readjust to the demands of my new status as a mother, and still achieve my dreams in life, especially when no one knows the truth and it is taboo to talk about these subjects. A teenager needs more professional and adult help. God knows what happened, so I do not need to plead my case.

The toxic shame, inadequacy, insecurity, and the lack of trust and intimacy manifest in me as being withdrawn, self-sabotage, harsh criticism, creating a cycle of emotional disconnection. This feeling also led me not to trust easily. Triggering events occur when an argument arises or when one is being physically abused under the influence of alcohol. I was coerced and compelled to physical sexual aggressiveness, together with belittling statements.

I was led into dark emotions where I let my negative thoughts, beliefs, and behaviours reinforce feelings of inadequacy and unworthiness. I did not feel loved, a sense of belonging, joy, or empathy towards my past traumas. It wasn't always easy to come to terms with my feelings, or the lack of them. I could not hug or tell my children how much I love them. My emotions were honest from the root cause; it was hard, and I was cold towards them. Day after day, I'd see couples holding hands, sharing sweet moments, and my heart would feel empty. It was like an emotional wall between me and the rest of humanity. But over time, what seemed like a curse became self-acceptance.

Being unable to feel love doesn't mean living a life without emotions. Plenty of things still brought joy into my life, like friendship bonds stronger than any romance could offer, career accomplishments that filled me with pride, and sunsets so stunning that they made my heart flutter. These experiences remind me that one can be fulfilled without needing romantic love. Feeling loveless can be arduous, but it's not the end of the world.

Recognising what I have been going through is a milestone in itself. It's okay to feel out of touch with your emotions or find it challenging to express love. Being in an unhealthy relationship, with no communication or expressing how I felt about any situation that took place at home, even making decisions, became unheard of and lonely. Loneliness can result in an urge to seek attention, and having low self-esteem is an overall sense of self-worth, which is intimately connected to my need for validation.

Facing Domestic Violence: Breaking the Silence

I was constantly being coerced, being called to check up on me at all times of my whereabouts, and what I am doing. Jealousy and possessiveness, the constant aggressive behaviour towards me, including how he disrespected me when talking to me. The name-calling is how he belittled me. He treated me like a child in front of the children. The isolation from family and friends felt like I was lost in myself. I sat in front of that TV to keep myself occupied and became a couch potato, which was not healthy. But it made me feel good, eating and crying at the same time.

I could not speak about my feelings to anyone. Praying and crying out aloud to God made me feel at peace and gave me that inner strength to take one day at a time, which was all I needed to focus and move on with myself. I had to take care of the children and carry on like everything was normal, which I felt it was, but deep down, I was drowning in pain and anger. I always had a smile to face the world, that everything was okay. Attending church gave me the courage and strength to endure whatever situation. It's painful when the person you trusted to spend your life with breaks you, then acts like you are the issue for the pain. He was unbothered watching me lose my mind over his destructive behaviours. I lost myself and realised I was fighting for something that was destroying me.

Whenever I felt like giving up, I found my strength in God. He was my saviour and Grace. I joined an NPO called Hands of Hope, where I was nominated as the secretary, but I felt awkward sharing my story. I had to build the courage and trust in my environment before sharing my story. I was in a safe space. I was embarrassed and ashamed that people would get to know what took place behind closed doors that were meant to be shut from the world. I was living in fear and shame.

I had to educate women afraid to speak about their daily situation. My story is for the women who stayed too long, for the ones still questioning their worth. For the ones who feel guilty walking away, you are not weak for leaving, you are not selfish for choosing yourself, and you are definitely not alone. Healing is messy and freedom is scary, but your peace is worth every step. You can be a catalyst for change when you are healed and whole. Your story can inspire and bring hope to others in the same situation.

Women of domestic abuse remain under the radar because they are ashamed that they have chosen to stay in a relationship with an abusive partner. Both culturally and socially, women are sensitive to the judgement they fear from others, whether they are suffering physical abuse, emotional abuse, or both. Reporting the perpetrator's behaviour would involve revealing embarrassing and humiliating details they would rather never discuss, especially if they have been enduring this treatment for years. There comes a time when you realise you don't have to keep rewriting your story that was never meant to be yours. You pack your truth, dignity, and every last ounce of courage and walk away, not because it was easy, but staying would have cost me my life.

I had to build my confidence to share my story. Breaking my silence could prevent other women from falling victim to the violence and empower them to speak out. We can create a society that not only listens but acts. Let's raise our voices instead of staying silent. Let us create a world free from the shackles of abuse. Let us prioritise our wellbeing, embark on a journey of self-discovery, and build a future filled with resilience, happiness, and fulfilment.

Life has taken me on this journey to be a voice for the voiceless, so I can rise from brokenness and still have grace beyond the shame and disgrace. I can still find beauty in brokenness, build myself, and encourage others. My road with no destination now is my road to success, where I can achieve my goals with beautiful scenery in front of me. I can see the beauty within myself and create a safe and empowered space for myself and other women who endure this pain.

Take me back to when laughter was endless, and my dreams were bigger than my fears.

Rebuilding Identity in Christ

As I grew stronger in my **faith,** it has allowed me to **gain** my inner strength. With **faith**, I do not feel alone. It also helped me give back and serve the less fortunate. My journey has helped me explore how faith informs, guides, and sustains my understanding of purpose in life. I felt the presence of God who sacrificed Himself for humanity's redemption (John 3:16). This love provides a foundation for self-worth and how I identify with Christ. God's love is not based on past mistakes but on His grace, which has helped me free myself from guilt and shame.

This scripture serves as a primary means through which GOD has chosen to reveal Himself and His purposes to us. According to Jeremiah 29:11, "For I know the plans I have for you, declares the Lord, plans to prosper and not for evil, to give you a future and a hope." It is a vital framework through which we discover, understand, and live out our purpose. It helps me connect to the community and my inner workings.

As we navigate life's difficulties, we often seek strength beyond ourselves. We turn to our faith and find comfort in knowing Christ supports us in our struggles. The Bible reminds us that our strength comes from Him, enabling us to persevere through trials and challenges. We can face whatever comes our way by grounding ourselves in His word. In our collective journey, we can uplift one another and lean on Christ, who strengthens us in our moments of need.

Philippians 4:13, "I can do all things through Christ who strengthens me," inspired me by reminding myself daily that through faith in Christ, we are empowered to overcome every obstacle. It is not about our strength but the strength we find in Him, which is limitless and always available. "Finally, be strong in the Lord and in his mighty power." – **Ephesians 6:10**.

This reminds me that my strength is not from my efforts but through reliance on the Lord's might. It encourages us to seek His strength daily and invites us to don the armour of God as we face life's battles.

Endurance is a crucial aspect of our Christian faith. As we face trials, we must learn to persist through difficulties rather than merely surviving them. The Bible consistently highlights endurance and its importance in our spiritual journey. We build character and hope by training ourselves to maintain faith even in tough times. Together, we can embrace the challenges before us, knowing that our ability to endure strengthens our belief and deepens our relationship with God. We are encouraged to view our trials as opportunities for growth. This call to joy in the face of hardships reminds us that endurance leads to maturity and completeness in our faith.

When faced with challenges and struggles in life, it is often hard to find the strength and hope to carry on. "God is our refuge and strength, a very present help in trouble," Psalm 46:1. This verse reminds us that no matter what we are going through, God is always there for us. He is our haven, anchor in the storm, and source of strength and hope.

When life becomes overwhelming and complicated, it can be tempting to feel alone and helpless. But as believers, we have the unshakeable knowledge that we are never truly alone. God's love provides us with the strength and hope we need to face any challenges that come our way.

God's love is a powerful force that anchors us in times of trouble. It is a constant presence in our lives, providing comfort and support when we need it the most. When we feel weak, His love gives us the strength to persevere. When we feel lost, His love guides us back to the right path.

In God's love, we find solace and peace. It is a love that is unwavering, never changing or diminishing. It is a love that knows no bounds and is always available. No matter what we are going through, we can find strength in knowing that we are deeply loved by a God greater than any obstacle.

God's love is not just a feeling but a transformative power. It can change us from the inside out, giving us the courage to face our fears and the confidence to overcome our weaknesses. With God's love as our anchor, we can weather any storm and emerge stronger than before.

Turning to God can offer a guiding light in times of darkness and despair. The knowledge that there is a divine plan and purpose can bring comfort and a renewed sense of hope. Believing in a mighty God allows individuals to trust that things will get better, even when circumstances seem impossible.

Furthermore, God's unwavering love and grace are sources of inspiration. Knowing that a higher power is watching over and guiding us can instil a deep sense of purpose and motivation. It reminds us that we are never alone and that there is always a reason to keep moving forward.

God's unconditional love and forgiveness also provide a wellspring of hope. No matter what mistakes or failures we may have encountered, knowing that God's love is always present allows us to find the strength to rise above adversity. It encourages us to learn and grow from our experiences and to never give up on ourselves or others.

A deeply personal **journey** of **healing**, forgiveness, finding peace with my father after his passing, and the profound ways **healing** continues beyond the physical realm. My world fell apart after my dad's passing. It's a love that runs deep, and I genuinely cherish it. However, it's essential to acknowledge that my relationship with my dad, like many father-child dynamics, can be complex. My dad was my pillar of strength.

Beacon of hope and a catalyst for change

I could not bond with my children at first, because they were conceived in pain—stitched from a season of trauma, not tenderness. Their presence reminded me of what I had survived, not what I had dreamt of. It was like trying to hold sunlight in a storm. Similar to singing a lullaby when your own voice has forgotten the melody. However, healing has a quiet enchantment. Over time, it was as if my heart, once wrapped in thorns, began to soften. And in that softening, I began to see them not as shadows of my past. But as echoes of possibility. They were never the trauma. The seeds were dropped into broken soil, waiting patiently for me to water them with my conscious presence.

And one day, I did. When I proactively found myself and began living consciously rather than numb and suppressed. I reached for them, not as a woman full of answers, but as one willing to feel. Willing to return. And in that return, I found something sacred: the invisible thread between our heartbeats began to hum. A rhythm I had missed, but never lost. That's the beauty of love born from pain—it does not vanish. It just waits for you to be ready to see it without the filter of fear.

And now? Every laugh, every hug, every "Mom" is no longer a reminder of what broke me. But what helped stitch me back together. I chose to survive and become a guiding light for others who are lost. I built the skill set. I crafted the voice. I turned my wounds into a compass. And I chose, daily, to shine, not because life was easy, but because someone else needed to see the light.

I became a beacon of hope—a catalyst for change. And if I could rise from the rubble, bleeding, trembling, unsure, and still become someone who sparks transformation in others, so can you. You don't need a perfect past to make a powerful impact. You need the courage to begin again—with trembling hands and a willing heart.

Patricia Duval

- Founder of PD Feeding Scheme NPC
- DIRECTOR of PD Training
- I am honoured to have received the Wonder Women's Award 2023.
- I am honoured to have received an award for the Premium Gala Award 2024

I was born and raised in the vibrant town of Wentworth, Durban. My passion lies in helping and feeding people in need in disadvantaged communities. As a young child, I grew up understanding the value of what I had. I ate whatever was on my plate, never questioning if it was enough, and wore what my parents could afford, knowing it was given with love and sacrifice. Gratitude was not what I learnt later in life. It was instilled in me through experience. I was raised to see the wealth in a meal prepared with love, in clothes given through sacrifice, in the small, steady offerings. I firmly believe charity begins at home, having that extra plate of food that I can help someone ensure they don't go to bed hungry.

I have vast experience in the training and safety sector. As I look toward the future, I celebrate the accomplishments of helping people in need. I firmly believe in the power of self-love, self-acceptance and self-care as essential elements for women's empowerment. Together we can raise awareness and build a brighter tomorrow. Don't be afraid to dream big; find the courage to pursue your dreams. Be the best version of yourself.

The War Within: My Fight for Power

Introduction

My name is Jeffrey Newman. You may refer to me as "Jeff." I am not the guy who has it all figured out. I am just a regular person who has been through hell and back; somehow, I am still standing. My story is not about perfect health or a smooth ride. No, it is about a brutal war I fought inside myself. A fight I almost lost, but one I refused to give up on.

My story is about chaos, pain, and the idea that my worst moments can become my greatest strength. It is about realising that my scars are not signs of weakness. They are badges of honour. And it is about our Beacon of Hope; honest, raw, undeniable HOPE.

I want to tell you this because I have experienced and found out what "broken" looks like. To feel like giving up was my only option. But I also know that deep inside, a fire is waiting to be reignited. This is about that fire. That power. That unbreakable spirit that refuses to die.

Ironically, many of us can relate to these emotions, not in my story but in yours.

My Mess, My Message

Let me start by saying, "I am not perfect." I will not claim to be. I grew up in Montreal, Canada, in the late 1950s and early 1960s. My family? Mom and Dad are a history lesson. My dad, Morris, survived five concentration camps.

I can only imagine that watching his entire family being slaughtered in Auschwitz damaged the boy I called "My father." And the resilience, resourcefulness, vulnerability, and radical acceptance that I took away from his traumatic tragedy. It's in my DNA. My mom, Rina, was luckier and fled from Israel, seeking safety in Canada with nothing but hope and stubbornness. Growing up, I was sweet, curious, and rambunctious. Like you,

I am full of energy and mistakes. I played sports, clueless about girls, and "tasted" life like a giant playground. I was popular, confident, and reckless. Later in my teens, pot, Boone Farms wine, and a whole lot of trouble, I was, in my mind, the king of chaos. But deep down, I felt something was not right.

Inside me, there was a storm brewing. Who knew I was facing a calamity only my creator could have known?

I was an average student in school, never the smartest or worst. I just wanted to keep up with the subjects and be liked and independent. But I was also hiding something. A deep, dark secret. I hallucinated it was my "not knowing." My uncertainty. All the battles, the waves of depression, anxiety, and energy that were approaching me. For example, when life creeps up on you, we say, "Where did the time go?"

I was young, spirited, and on top of the world, clueless, while working my way towards visiting my creator.

I never doubted myself getting into college. Yeah, I had a soccer scholarship with the University of Maryland. The chaos was calling me. I chased semi-professional soccer in Israel, thinking I was chasing greatness, but I was running from myself. I was living on the edge and living fast, secretly dying, and loving every second of it.

When I finally returned to America, I had nothing to show for it: no money, a steady job, or a plan. But I had a dream. A vision. Something I clung to like a lifeline. I started my first business, Newco Data, in 1986. It was my ticket out of the chaos. For 22 years, I built that company, worked my ass off, and believed I was unstoppable. Until one day, everything changed. "Me."

Bankruptcy, heartbreak, nervous breakdowns, loss of identity, my life was a mess. I was battered and broken. I felt like I was drowning in a sea of failure. I was convinced I would never bounce back.

Here's the thing I did. Failure is not the enemy. I know now that the universe told me, "I was not done yet." In retrospect, every disaster, heartbreak, and setback was just a setup for my comeback.

And then, at the age of 52, life threw me a new punch, a diagnosis of a person challenged with bipolar disorder. For years, I would feel the waves of those highs of energy and creativity, those lows of despair and exhaustion. But now, I had a name for it. Personally, it was a relief. Freedom. It was a call to action.

Like an active volcano, that moment changed everything. I realised my chaos, my pain, was raw material. It could be used as fuel. It was the blueprint for a new life. One filled with purpose, love, and abundance.

Almost everyone I know has an inner critic. I do. Meet Evelyn, the wise Owl. My emotional intelligence whispers truths of vulnerability and patience.

And Aiden, the cunning Fox. My strategic AI slicing through chaos, analysing, planning, turning storms into opportunities.

Together, they became my internal army. My secret weapons in the fight for my life. They taught me that resilience is not about never falling. It is about how fast you get up. How fiercely you fight. How boldly you believe in yourself.

Vicariously, I would be walking and living my father's death walk. I offer you my story to make it yours. Because here's a secret, it is your chaos that is your greatest gift. Your wounds. Your badges of honour. Your failures. The clay from which you master your resilience.

Here is the art of the deal: if you are tired of feeling broken, exhausted, or stuck, think about the fight not being over. Think of it as the beginning. And I am here to encourage you that sometimes what we think is not who we are.

There is a reason to fight—The Three Ps That Will Save Your Life.

Let's be real. Life does not care if you are tired, scared, or broken. It will punch you so hard you wonder if you are still standing. And, if I were standing, it would punch me down again.

My truth was, "Jeff, you have two choices. Stay down or get up and fight like hell.

Here is a question: if you have been through a catastrophe, close to death, mental collapse, addiction, trauma, you may already know the answer. Is a fight mandatory? Are you made for more?

Evelyn and Aiden say, "Yes," and will have your back.

Our pains are not a warning. And not a "dress rehearsal." The alarm clock rings in your face, screaming, "Wake up!". Stop hiding. Stop numbing. Feel it all because that is where real healing begins.

Real Talk: My Pain Was My Prison, the First "P."

Let me take you inside my darkest hour. I was in bed for hours a day, buried under the covers in a dark room, sweating, trembling, crying, paralysed. I felt like I was already dead. I was just waiting for the final curtain, my last hurrah. Every day was a battle just to get out of bed, face the world, and breathe.

I will confidently say the truth nobody wants to admit, "accepting that pain was the first step to breaking free."

I finally looked at myself in that dark room while Evelyn and Aiden fuelled my thinking and said, "Enough." I knew I could not keep living like that. I had a lot of work ahead of me. No shortcuts. No fighting back, no excuses. The first step was to start getting out of bed. Simple. Right? Perhaps so, but not easy. Just that, getting out of bed. For me, it was everything. I told myself, "Just sit up. Just swing your legs over the side." One tiny, brutal step. At times, I did not make it past taking the covers from over my head. Crying, sweating, and screaming took on the theme "Someday."

The road to someday will always lead me to a town called "Nowhere."

Again, the strength I regained kept showing up.

You sow what you reap, and slowly, painfully, I built a habit. I celebrated every tiny victory. By getting out of bed, turning on the light, and stepping into the shower, I realised that practising this "Pain" was my artillery and became my lifeline.

And, you know what? That small act of "Practice" was the courage to get out of bed. It gave me the momentum to break the chains that I thought were handcuffing me to the prison bars.

The Second "P."

Over many weeks and months, jumping out of my "pain comfort zones" for recovery became my ritual, taking my mental health challenges to a new level for the opportunity to stop living in my darkness, and jumping into an illuminated room of freedom.

My truth is that our pain is our most excellent teacher. I became the most outstanding student, facing my bloody, ugly, and relentless challenges. The rebirth of those positive emotions, I thought, was lost because of my beliefs about being a victim of my circumstances. Propelling the victories were the riches I acquired because of my radical acceptance.

I will reiterate my belief in taking the pain and practising it. Accept being knocked down, maybe knocked out, but the champion is not the one who never falls. They are the ones who get back up over and over until they are unrecognisable and unbreakable.

Finally, Patience. The Third "P."

If you expect overnight miracles, you are fooling yourself. Healing is a marathon. A war of attrition. It is a slow, brutal, and worthwhile path to constant, never-ending improvement.

Trust the process. Because what comes from your uncertainties is not just recovery. It is a rebirth. You are forging a new identity in the fire, which takes time to awaken your giant within.

Breathe. Trust. Keep going. Your breakthrough is brewing.
Just do not rush it.

Chapter 3: Jumping into the Deep End—The Courage to Accept.

I will be blunt. Denial is a bitch. It is the sneakiest, most destructive lie we tell ourselves. It whispers, "You are fine, you got this," secretly sinking us into despair. For years, I danced with denial like it was my best friend. Pretending.

Hoping for my "freedom of doom" was overrated. I made all my actions a "Must." I finally ignited the courage I had convinced that I had lost, and jumped into a pool of radical acceptance, swimming my way across the Gulf of America!

The Liberation of 1945 from tyranny to the awakening of 2025.

At 52, I never expected my life would disappear. I was married, healthy, successful, a CEO, with multiple properties, plenty of material assets, vested in my retirement, and cash-rich. Living, again, the American dream. At least I thought I had these things. With losing everything initially, I discovered that not avoiding taking the pain turned out to be the impetus for gaining my pleasures.

My past fifteen years surprised me with medications, therapy, psychiatrists, medical doctors, hospitals, losses, tears, and threatening thoughts.

Many individuals chose to bend to these challenges. I swam in the opposite direction, swimming upstream as I witnessed many going downstream.

I took them on as challenges. I saw outrageous positive side effects. First, I revitalised my real Purpose. My "Why." Proving to myself that I never lost any of my internal greatness. I just was not releasing my genuine emotions.

I was born again as the Advocate, Coach, Speaker, Author, Influencer, and Confidant with Mental Health challenges. To be the messenger for teaching and guiding others, they can learn through example. I became the "Beacon of Hope" for those who wanted to help themselves.

Evelyn and Aiden referred to me as the "Cicada miracle." I would now be known again for my loud buzzing noises radiating wherever I go. Speaking engagements started to fill my calendar. High schools, colleges, universities, businesses, churches, synagogues, and conferences became my new platform. My corporate lifestyle was upstaged for a much more fulfilling replacement.

Gratefulness opened more possibilities now in all situations that I thought were impossible.

I focused on what I have, not what I did not have. Does this sound like a mishmash of clichés? It surely is. But I'll take it.

My new beginning became my trademark for welcoming this newfound stigma, which reads, "imperfectly perfect," on my upper left arm.

I do not see myself or anybody living with these diseases as dysfunctional. We simply have an alternate mindset. After sharing my experiences, I discovered that telling people where I am and what I am going through usually results in a transfer of feelings of inspiration, patriotism, and approval.

The spectators are in the stands, and I am on the playing court. Sharing my story has transformed how I see my disorder. It does not mean I will not feel negative feelings; it means understanding the ability to acknowledge and respect them. It also does not mean I will not face another obstacle. It means I will approach the next obstacle with my open heart and wide blue eyes, no matter how painful.

I keep repeating Winston Churchill's quote, "Pessimists see opportunities as challenges, whereas optimists see challenges as opportunities.

NO JOKE

I sometimes close my eyes and think back to my fifty-two-year-old self. I was there in my darkness with my demons, reinforcing myself that I'm worthless, alone, and unloved. So, I go up to myself with a hug because I do not feel so alone when "we" are feeling uncomfortable and vulnerable.

I yell, "Newman, you are okay. You are powerful, strong, and imperfectly perfect! You got this." I watch as I take all my vitality inward, releasing it in small breaths.

With laughter and excitement, I remind myself to "Keep on going. There are so many more to teach, comfort, and soothe." I look back for the last time, screeching and yelling as I wave goodbye, "See you around, Jeff Newman, you can and have been liberated out of your final death march."

My end is my beginning.

Jeff Newman

Jeff Newman is an inspiring entrepreneur, a dedicated father, and a loyal friend. As a passionate speaker, writer, and influencer, he is driven by a strong desire to contribute, grow, and bring value to the world. With unwavering positivity and a spirited approach, Jeff embraces each challenge enthusiastically and with pride. His inspiring journey reflects his commitment to making a meaningful difference, inspiring others to pursue their best selves and create lasting impact.

Finding Jesus in the Pain

I want to begin this chapter by acknowledging that we each have a story to tell, a testimony. My story is not unique; it is not about me, but it is unique to my Creator and entirely about Him. He is the one I had to learn to trust unconditionally, something I'm still learning every day, as human nature constantly urges us to take control.

Our Creator has a plan greater than we could ever imagine for each of our lives. He gives us the choice: to plan our own way or to step out in faith and trust Him, stepping into the future He has prepared for us.

I wish every person reading this would know that **your story matters**. It needs to be told. Someone needs to hear it. It may serve as a beacon of hope to someone else. Likewise, we must be open to listening to the stories of others. God sends people across our path for a reason. It may be to share your story or to hear theirs.

I have been deeply blessed by every person I've encountered. Each one, I believe, was a God-sent angel. From the moment I took my first breath, and that is precisely where I will begin the first miraculous breath of Liesel Viljoen (now Bredenkamp).

17 January 1980

Not many people can remember their first breath, but I can. Let me explain.

When you experience trauma and need hypnosis to address it, it's incredible how far back your subconscious mind can go. But to understand the depth of this, I need to start 18 years from my birth, to give you proper context.

18 November 1998

It was the last day of school, and my dear parents agreed to let all my friends come over for a "braai" (BBQ). We planned to celebrate the end of an era in my life, a chapter that had been truly blessed. I had great friends, a loving family, and many reasons to be thankful.

The day before, my dad showed me how to light the fire. After my last exam, I tried to light it myself but struggled, so I called him for help. As always, he came.

My mum and sister were busy in the kitchen preparing dinner. None of us knew that this simple act of help from Dad would trigger a day straight out of hell.

My dad was hijacked and shot five times in front of our home. He never lit that fire for me.

(Scripture: *"Even though I walk through the valley of the shadow of death, I will fear no evil, for you are with me..."* – Psalm 23:4)

We lived in South Africa, a breathtakingly beautiful country with an intense heartbeat. We had, sadly, become accustomed to crime. My mum had been hijacked two years earlier. We'd had multiple break-ins over the years. Too many incidents to name. But God's hand had always been over us. We had been protected. Not physically harmed. We always said, "It could've been worse."

Now, I realise that being exposed to trauma is not "okay" either. But even then, we knew **God had us.**

Back to that day

Seeing your father lying in a puddle of blood, in the rain, at the entrance of your home, is surreal. I remember looking down and seeing his pulse, literally the vein in his wrist, as his hand had been shot and the flesh was gone. His teeth had been shot out. His chest was bleeding from shrapnel. He had collapsed after being shot in both legs.

But on that day, I experienced a miracle.

I looked up and saw our front lawn full of people. It's vivid in my memory. But now, I know that was impossible. We lived in a secure complex. Only residents had access. Outsiders couldn't just stop and gather. No one worked from home in those days.

So, who were those people?

I believe they were angels.

I walked straight toward a peaceful, radiant woman who stood out among the crowd. Something pulled me to her. She gently asked, "Can I pray for you?" Through tears, I said, "Yes, please." I remember her prayer as if it happened yesterday.

When she finished, my sister came running to say the ambulance had gotten lost. When I looked up again, the lawn was nearly empty. Only a few people remained. It was surreal. I forced myself into action.

The ambulance finally arrived and took my dad to the hospital. What shocked me was how unlike TV it all was. My dad lay there, unattended, in the emergency. No one is rushing to help. It seemed like no one cared.

But again, God showed up.

Some dear family friends, doctors, made calls, and only then was my dad attended to.

While waiting, I met "Oom Tommy." In Afrikaans, "Oom" means "Uncle," a respectful title. He was calm and warm and asked what had happened. I told him everything. Then he shared his story: he and his wife were supposed to embark on a once-in-a-lifetime trip around South Africa. But that night, she'd been hit by a drunk driver and was in surgery.

He radiated such peace. No anger. No fear. Just trust in God.

That moment taught me something powerful: people may forget your words, but never forget how you made them feel.

"And the peace of God, which surpasses all understanding, will guard your hearts and your minds in Christ Jesus." – Philippians 4:7

She didn't survive. I wonder if he ever took that trip. But what he gave me was faith, and calmness remained. I wish I could thank him.

Gratitude

My dad survived. After months of rehabilitation and countless prayers, God gave us another 25 years with him. For that, I am forever grateful.

But trauma had changed me. Once a vibrant, outgoing young woman, I became unrecognisable. I was anxious, angry, scared. I clung to my parents and struggled through university and hostel life. Every phone call triggered panic. I snuck home more times than I can count. I withdrew socially.

Then I met a friend, Theresa, a God-sent angel. Her dad had also been shot that same year. But unlike mine, he didn't survive. He was hit only once. I felt overwhelmed with guilt and confusion. Why did mine survive and hers didn't?

I wrestled with God. "Why?" I asked again and again.

Now I know: **in a broken world, God has already won** even when it doesn't feel like it.

I realised the magnitude of our miracle. She helped me understand what it meant to be truly blessed. Her strength, her faith, is unmatched. She helped me heal. We're still friends today, though we live in different countries.

Finding my silver lining

I later saw a trauma counsellor, a minister trained in hypnotherapy. I still felt trapped in the trauma. Unable to forgive. Unable to move forward. In one session, he guided me back **to my birth**.

Yes, I know it sounds impossible. But with God, nothing is.

I was born via assisted delivery, the umbilical cord wrapped around my neck. In that session, I re-lived the moment I couldn't breathe and then the moment the cord was cut.

I screamed. In his office. The same scream I likely gave at birth. It was a release. My mother came running in. And the healing began.

Trauma triggers trauma. But healing is possible. Even at 45, I still see that healing is a lifelong journey.

I find the closer I stay to Jesus, the less power trauma has over me. *"Come to me, all you who are weary and burdened, and I will give you rest."* – Matthew 11:28

Purpose

Since moving to Australia, our faith has grown. It's no longer just about asking God to "keep us safe," but about walking with Him and building a genuine relationship. We read the Bible every day. We listen. We pray. We were even blessed to be baptised by the Holy Spirit. A prophetic prayer was spoken over our family, declaring that we would help others through Christ, who gave us life. I am also blessed with a beautiful family and two incredible boys who love God and live close to Him—what more could a girl ask for?

My husband and I prayed for years to discover our purpose. And here, in a foreign land we now call home, we founded **GraceWell Group**—a mission-driven business to build **wells** of hope, helping people grow and thrive.

I give all the praise to God.

You are not alone; God is with you. He sends angels in human form and may even choose to use you as one in someone else's life. Stay open to His blessings and be a beacon of hope.

Liesel Bredenkamp

My name is Liesel Bredenkamp, and first and foremost, I am a child of God. I was born in South Africa and raised in a loving home, where despite the challenges of living in a country marked by crime, my childhood was filled with joy, hope, and dreams. In high school, I met the man of my dreams, and at 23 I was blessed to marry him. Together we have been gifted with two beautiful, sporty boys who fill our lives with pride and laughter. In 2009, we took a leap of faith and immigrated to Adelaide, Australia, to begin a new chapter, one led by trust in our Creator and a desire to walk closely with Him as a family.

The House That Held My Screams

I always hated being a child and wanted to grow up fast to be a part of adult conversation and their secrets. As an only child, there were many things I didn't know about, although I was always curious. My family kept a lot of secrets from me. Some were just light, harmless, but some were more serious. I remember feeling frustrated as a child, extremely loved but not very relatable, because of the considerable age gap between me and the rest of the family.

I wished upon shooting stars to have many kids when I get married. I am blessed and grateful that my wish was granted, and I have two children - my moon and my star. I also promised myself that I would not keep any secrets from my children like my family did with me. The main reason for writing these feelings is to let them know everything I remember. I wouldn't want to die without sharing my life story with them.

When I was little, I learned that some things made the most sense to keep to myself. If we didn't talk about things, they didn't happen, even if they had happened already. Whilc I sensed my family kept their day-to-day secrets. I kept a secret far more burdensome. It started when my stepbrother started molesting me.

My parents thought it was okay to leave me with him, as he was supposed to be a protector I could trust and that he would protect me when they were away. I didn't mean to keep it a secret, but I was so naive that I didn't even realise what a podophile he was. When it first started, I had no idea I was being molested. I was just confused. My Family didn't talk about things like that. Maybe they never thought it could happen in our family.

It was late at night. I held my breath and frantically tried to wrap myself in blankets without being too obvious. I had heard stories where men would become violent when they knew you knew. So, I was careful. He walked through my bed and stood beside it. He would gently stroke me to see if I was awake. I could feel his hands go over my bra, and sometimes I would move just enough to scare him. Sometimes it worked, and sometimes he kept trying.

He usually got what he wanted because I was scared to speak up. Every night, he would walk to my bed and breathe heavy enough that I could hear his breath on his beard. And he would lie next to me, touching my breasts and playing with himself. His lips on the back of my neck felt like thorns. Some days, he would leave after playing with my body for a bit, but other days, he would keep touching me until he released his buildup. It started when I was 10 and ended when I turned 15 or 16. I did a pretty good job handling it for that long, but it didn't end well.

For ages, I kept that secret inside. The secret of something so horrific that I couldn't even comprehend. All that guilt, anger, and confusion I felt in my stomach. I felt it in my mind. I felt it in my body. I felt it in my soul, and then the secret exploded when he raped me.

When the glowing baby girl of the family ended up in the hospital, the news landed in the local neighbourhood. And then my family tried to tell lies to cover it up. If you don't share your secret, people will tell you your secrets, even if they are painful. But the story doesn't end there; more and more secrets were kept from me, and they have ruined me. It crushed my soul. I'm sick of the secrets. Give me some light and peace.

He ruined me and broke me into a million pieces. He changed me for the rest of my life. He changed the way I looked at people. He changed the way I looked at my own family. He changed the meaning of a brother for me. He changed the way I grew up. He changed everything about me. He changed me drastically. He was my abuser, and that's how I will always recognise and address him.

What broke me more was when Mum accepted him back after a year or so. Why did she take him back? Did she even think of me when she received him back? Did she know how it affected me when she accepted him back? These questions remain and haunt me to this day. Whenever I tried to speak to her about it, she encouraged me to be a good person and forgive him. How can I forgive the person who committed such a terrible crime? Why was she teaching me to be a good person when I didn't commit any crime?

Unless you consider hiding the abuse as a crime, and if that's the case, I'm sure there are many innocent victims out in this world who are criminals. God help us. My mental health worsened over the years when I was young. I couldn't eat or drink properly. I had no self-confidence. I didn't want to socialise. I had no intention of living. I wanted to go. I just wanted to set myself free. I tried and tried, but an angel looked after me every time. Every single time I wanted to end it, I was saved by my guardian angel and was given another chance.

Eventually, I gave up on even trying, and after failed attempts, it was time to start speaking up about my truth. As soon as I was coming back to a somewhat normal life, my mum took me to a counselling session to bring some peace to my mind, but some things are just not easy to talk about at all. Anyway, I spent most of my teen years covering for him.

I took the brunt of the emotional trauma until I could no longer carry it. I finally spoke with a

counsellor. That's a story in itself, but it backfired. It went through my parents' social circle like fire. And at 17, I decided to leave home. I was homeless, nowhere to go, with nothing in my pockets. After spending a few nights on the streets, I finally contacted one of my friends. God bless those people who saved me at that time.

I was at my friend's house for only a few days until my mum came to take me back. And returned home with her because, I guess, I couldn't bear her crying in her mental state. She looked shattered. I had one condition: I wouldn't stay in our house if he was there. Mum promised me to get rid of him, but needed some time. That time never came. I was 19 and I had to get out of jail. I never spoke to him in that house again, but his presence was enough to make me uncomfortable.

It was like living in a fancy prison. I had to leave India, so I decided to move to Australia. I felt alive leaving that house. I finally did it. I still get asked why I don't try to testify in court and why I don't try to confront him or attempt to expose him. I don't need to do anything about it. The universe will give him what he deserves. I know it in my heart, and it's my truth. Just because I haven't shamed or confronted him directly doesn't mean the universe can't hear me.

In the quiet moments of my day, when the world quietens and my thoughts become loud, I accept the hard truth that they don't stand where I stand, so they'll never know. It's a silent lament, and understanding that not everyone can honestly see the depth of my experiences until they have walked in my shoes. People catch glimpses of my life. They see the smiles and achievements, but don't see the bridges I've crossed, the silent battles I've fought, the lonely nights I've spent filled with doubt and despair. They don't know the weight of my burdens, the scars from my struggles, the resilience I've had to muster to keep going. It's easy to judge from a distance, to think you know someone's story just because you've seen a chapter. But the pages of my life are filled with struggles and triumphs that are uniquely mine.

Each step I take is a testament to the resilience I've built, the pain I've endured, and the strength I've discovered. And until you walk in my shoes, you can't possibly understand the emotional journey that has shaped who I am. When someone says, "I get it," I know they mean well, but do they really? Can they feel the sting of my childhood torture, the exhaustion of my constant failures? They can't honestly know my painful journey until they stand where I stood and feel the ground shake beneath their feet with doubt.

"You don't stand where I stand, so you'll never know." This phrase echoes in my mind when I'm judged, when my choices are questioned, when my struggles are minimised. It's a reminder that genuine empathy goes beyond words. It requires stepping into someone else's shoes, seeing the world through their eyes, and feeling their heartache as if it were your own. I've learned to find solace in my strength and recognise the power within me that comes from facing my challenges. I've learned that I don't need everyone to understand me. I must keep pushing forward and crossing these bridges, no matter how daunting they seem. We all walk our paths, shaped by unique experiences and challenges. And while others may not fully understand our journey, it is ours to embrace and navigate. Ultimately, this personal journey defines us, strengthens us, helps us evolve, and makes us who we are.

I needed to write this to bring courage in telling this truth and to serve healing and justice to others. I lived in a prison built not by walls, but by silence—silence that whispered I was powerless, invisible, broken. The very people who should have been my protectors became my tormentors. I was forced to breathe the same air, walk the same floors, carry the same name as the ones who stole my childhood. That pain could have swallowed me whole. It almost did.

BUT I SURVIVED, and so can you.

Not because the world was kind to me, or because justice came swiftly. I survived because somewhere deep inside, beneath the shame, the fear, and the endless nights of despair, a small flicker of light refused to die. It was hope—fragile, trembling, but fierce. I took my shattered pieces and gathered them with trembling hands. I let my story bleed raw onto the pages of my life, refusing to hide the scars that many wanted to ignore. From the coma of my trauma, I woke—not as a victim, but as a warrior. Each wound became a testament to resilience, each tear a seed for growth.

Today, I am a **Beacon of HOPE** for those trapped in darkness, a catalyst for change in a world that often turns its back on broken souls. My pain has become my power, my silence transformed into a roar that demands justice, compassion, and healing. I speak because I refuse to let my story be buried beneath shame.

This is not just my story. It is the story of every survivor who has been forced to live alongside their pain, who has felt unseen and unheard. If you are reading this and carrying a burden too heavy to bear, know this—you are not alone. Light is beyond the shadow, strength beyond the brokenness, and a future waiting to be reclaimed. Step forward and grab it with both hands.

The past shaped me, but it does not define me. **I am more than what was done to me**. I am proof that even from the deepest wounds, a life of hope, courage, and change can rise.

Seema Anonymous

- Resilience is the ability to rise after devastation.
- Grit is the perseverance to keep going, even when everything says stop.
- Compassion is a heart tuned to the pain of others and the will to serve.
- Courage is speaking the truth even when her voice shakes.
- Vision is seeing possibilities where others see ruins.
- Empowerment is using her voice to help others reclaim theirs.

Seema is more than a survivor—she is a force of transformation. Instead of letting her story end silently, she turned her suffering into a powerful catalyst for change. After immigrating to a new country with nothing but her courage and faith, Seema built a thriving business from the ground up. Today, she is a successful entrepreneur and advocate for trauma survivors around the world. Seema's journey is a living testament to the human spirit's capacity for resilience, grit, and unshakable hope. Her voice is tender and fierce—a lighthouse for those still navigating stormy seas.

Introducing the HEART of Sonam's Expression

In this compelling section of *Beacon of Hope: A Catalyst for Change*, we are honoured to feature the evocative poems and artwork of Sonam—a creative soul whose pen and brush speak the language of resilience, healing, and truth.

Each piece shared here is rooted in Sonam's experiences—moments of challenge, awakening, and deep introspection—transformed into art that now reaches out to hold the hands of others walking their own path. Her work is more than creative expression; it is a balm for weary hearts, a whisper of strength for those on the edge of giving up, and a radiant light for anyone searching for meaning amid pain.

Through poetic verse and visual storytelling, Sonam reminds us that beauty can rise from brokenness and that even the softest voice can echo loudly in the hearts of many. Her contribution is an offering—raw, honest, and radiant—gifted to humanity, hoping to ignite courage, comfort, and inspiration in all who encounter it.

My Salvation Testimony

Hearing Your voice, I knew I was the one You were seeking.
Your love was evident, to my heart, You were speaking.
For You are the Father, and You give new life
Hearing that message, I was released from anguish and strife.
You were working to heal my broken heart.

Putting back together the pieces torn apart

I held onto Your promise. I am close to the broken-hearted
and those who are crushed in spirit.

Your hand moved miraculously to rescue me from the pit

You say those that are bowed down, I speedily lift

Your love was further demonstrated as I received understanding. Your Son, Jesus, was sent for my salvation, a precious gift.

I was encouraged to hear. You lifted Peter out from sinking in the deep water. I had confidence to rely on You as a daughter.

I decided to move away on my own
But with You by my side, I wouldn't be alone

My world was turned upside down

However, You were the rock upon which my feet were found. You sent a person to confirm Your heart, attitude, and Jesus loves me.

Tears flowed from my eyes. Your love was clearly seen, a relational living God reaching down for me.

I put my hopes in You and asked You to speak instead of relying on behaving recklessly.

You said to be careful of the company you keep and not to let negative thoughts have a stronghold over me.

You also dried my tears and gave advice so dear.

Letting me know to be with someone who loves You more than he loves me, as You will teach him how to love and treat me

Now I can see that's how it is meant to be since You sent my husband Ben to love and cherish me.

Through that process, You kept me safe in perilous situations,
Winning me over with Your gentle persuasions.

You heard my heart cry, changed my life against all odds, did You defy
You led me out from idols, new age and sin.
You have been with me all along, surrounding me with grace.

Blessing me with the opportunity to know You and seek Your face
You forgive, protect, provide, heal, deliver, comfort and guide.

Your truths permeate my life, as I learn to abide.
Divine connections and treasured friends through Your church, I have met.
Being with You, there are no regrets.

For on Me before the foundations of the world Your heart was set.
You have given me a new identity, made me a new creature from the past.

I am set free and have been purchased from the world by Jesus' shed blood. Now, redeemed, He can do for You what He has done for me.

Inspired on 28/02/2020

His Love

In a prison of torment, once confined
I was in a dire state of anguish and pain.

But Your love washed over me like refreshing rain.
The love of the Father is love like no other.

Father God, You made the greatest sacrifice giving Jesus, freedom, victory and life, the chains of the past I now leave behind.

Your grace has allowed me to cast insurmountable mountains into the sea.
Your word has replaced destructive lies and brought forth the enemy's demise.

You have lifted my head as Your beloved child and caused me to rise.
My heart rejoices and is glad as I testify to Your goodness.

You have given my soul wholeness and rest.
The depths of my being have received healing; in Your abundant mercy, I am blessed!

Inspired on 28/12/2022

Lover of My Soul

You are the lover of my soul, piecing me back together, making every part of me whole. Through You, Lord Jesus, I have eternal life, a new beginning and a fresh start.

You rescued me from the pit with Your exceeding love. You endured the cross for me, Lord Jesus, going to such a great length.

You are my salvation and my strength.

Your love knows no bounds, reaches higher than the heavens and deeper than the ocean's depths, mending my broken heart and bringing life to the places that were once dead.

You've redeemed, ransomed and transformed my life through every drop of blood you shed. I praise You for the victory You purchased for me when You bled.

Thank You for Your faithfulness, Lord Jesus, my Father and Friend
You have released me from the evil of the past through Your steadfast mercy and grace.

You are worthy, Lord Jesus, of all honour and praise!

Inspired on 20/8/2022

Precious and Priceless

Precious and priceless in Your sight
You sent Your Son, Lord Jesus, to rescue me from death and demise. No one else could save me from my plight.

You rejoice over me, I am Your delight.
You adopted me as Your child.

You have preserved me as I sought refuge in You, Most High.
You always keep Your promises.

You're always on my side, encouraging me to keep moving forward. You equip me with Your authority and power to fight the good fight in the darkest places of my life You have brought.

Your radiant light, You have written my name on the palm of Your hands.
You have redeemed my life with a good plan.

Inspired on 28/08/2022

Purity of Your Love

No longer am I plagued by pain, engulfed in a helpless situation.
As Your unfailing love has rescued me and exceeded all my expectations, distress and desperation no longer have a relentless grip on me

As beloved Lord Jesus paid with His blood and His life for my victories, Your love, oh Lord, is life-giving and has no end.

I am adored by the King of kings and Lord of lords.
You paid a price for me, Father God, which I could never afford.

Your love is a healing balm to my soul, making me whole.
Your Word is mending my broken heart that was torn.

With kindness and strength, my life You adorn.
You have been rejoicing over me since I was born.

Always faithful and ever by my side, no longer am I forsaken or forlorn. You carry me when I am weary and worn.

In Your loving embrace, Father God, I am secure.
The purity of Your love leaves me in reverence and awe.

Inspired on 30/12/2022

Living for the King

You are my life source, my Lord, my everything, my all in all from dusk until dawn, breaking fetters, restoring my joy and gladness.

You have brought me to a place of security and belonging, making obsolete the pain of isolation and once being forlorn, mending the brokenness inside, where I was downcast and torn.

You have given me a garment of praise, strength in place of being trampled on

You have built steady foundations in my life, and gifted me beauty for ashes, and companionship instead of heartache and strife.

My Comforter, my Hope, my Joy, my Song

Your love and goodness, I will live in and reflect, you have called me Your own, Your daughter to whom Your kindness shows forth.

You have made me in Your image, through Your priceless sacrifice, Lord. You have prized my value, beauty, and worth.

You caused me to rise up, and as Your daughter, a child of God, the light of the world and salt of the earth.

You have given me authority and victory over the power of the enemy, and placed Your purpose within me before birth.

There's no comparison to knowing You and being captivated by Your love. You have set me free, with You I am no longer bound.

Through Your grace, I have been raised by Jesus, my Saviour and Your beloved Son.

I lift my voice and praise to You, Oh Lord, You have resurrected my life, with your love, no longer dead and depleted, I am more than a conqueror through Christ.

Your faithfulness has delivered me from destruction. I am

protected and sheltered by Your kindness.

Your mercy has restored me through Your precious blood that for me was sacrificially shed, no longer am I diminished by the darkness, walking in dread.

Inspired on 27/02/2024

No Longer Empty

My life is no longer empty or hollow because I know who holds my present, future and tomorrow. You are the One Lord Jesus I choose to follow.

You have eased my grief, suffering and sorrow.
You paid for and sealed my healing with Your blood.

A covenant promise You've made for me, magnifying Your love

You are El Shaddai, the God of freedom who gives generously, whoever the Son sets free is free indeed.

You have released me from captivity and raised me from a place of brokenness in humility.

The Lord Most High Who supplies healing for my wounds, a soothing balm which darkness cannot defy.

You sustained me when I could not walk.

You are the strength of my soul, my Defender, my Deliverer who has saved me, by Your precious blood, Lord Jesus. I have been bought.

You sit on the throne; the enemy has been defeated, and no longer am I shackled by pain and havoc Satan wrought.

Through the power of Your sacrifice, the evil I have endured throughout life has been nullified.

You rejoice with me, Lord Jesus, thank You, You died to give me a life of victory, and because of You, I am empowered to live this life more abundantly.

Inspired in October 2022

In Love and Mercy

In love and mercy, You incline Your ear to tear down My fears

In times of turmoil, You hear my cries and wipe my tears.

When I am crushed and broken, there You are, comforting me, ever near.

In a world of chaos and confusion, Your Word remains true, steadfast and clear, directing me in the way I should go.

Holy Spirit, Your loving presence uplifts and restores me.

My wonderful and faithful Counsellor, with me You dwell.

You are my hiding place of refreshment and rest.

In You I confide when I am burdened and hard pressed.

Lord, in Your gracious and merciful presence, I am encouraged and helped.

Father, You are the Good Shepherd, strong and worthy, with infallible love. You have faithfully held and carried me.

Inspired on **16/04/2025**

You Hear My Heart

You hear my heart when I don't speak a word.

My silence is deafening, but You hear my desires and distresses within the depths of my being. Your love surrounds me, and I am held in Your perfect peace and protection.

You encompass me with compassion, kindness and affection. My tears, You have gathered and numbered like pearls within a precious collection.

Inspired on 21/05/2025

Beauty for Ashes

Your love is saving my soul,

Rescuing me from destruction.

Your life-giving words provide me with priceless instruction.

You govern my life with care and kindness.

Your grace and strength have empowered me to break chains and fetters.

You have transformed my life, with beauty for ashes.

You adorn me with a crown of victory, I offer You praise and thanksgiving.

I am grateful for the renewing of my mind, Lord Jesus, which has enriched my life and been a tremendous blessing.

Inspired on 13/11/2022

Beauty for Ashes - Painting 2023

Sonam Rifkin

Sonam Rifkin's creativity expresses her worship and adoration for Lord Jesus Christ to glorify and serve Him. It is a privilege and honour for her to share her writing and visual arts with others as a testament of His transformational love and everlasting goodness, especially in her life. The Holy Spirit inspires the pieces she produces as she partners with Him and her faith journey, which the Word of God can underpin.

Who Told You?

Introduction

Compelling, Confident, Energetic, Successful, Connected, Clear-Headed, Fearless, Attractive, and Comfortable in one's skin. How often have you desired that these traits would simply wash over you, allowing you to wake up daily as an unstoppable version of yourself?

For years, I suffered from not knowing my true identity. I sometimes wondered if God could achieve anything with a broken emotional mess like me.

The Mysterious Envelope

Growing up in a Christian home, I was exposed to Christian Bible studies. I signed up to do a Bible correspondence course. It was in the morning like any other day. I was watching TV with Mum when I received an A4 envelope addressed to me.

I saw my name, so I thought it was my Bible correspondence and hurried to open it. What dropped out of the envelope got my heart pumping, and my palms sweating. Suddenly, a migraine started. There was no time to think.

In a split second, 'ONLY ANGEL' caught my attention. Oh gosh!!

Faster than speedy Gonzales, but not to make it too obvious, I grabbed the envelope and ran to put it in my room. I hid the envelope in my underwear drawer, for even if Mum had become suspicious, she would not have opened that drawer, so now, at least, the envelope would remain in the drawer until it was time for me to go to bed.

From as early as breakfast, my only thought was, *"Can time speed up? Why is this day dragging?"* I kept myself busy by helping around the house. I did everything to keep my mind busy, but it didn't lessen the distraction waiting for me. I was ready to go to bed when I realised what was inside the A4 envelope.

Finally, bedtime arrived. I made my way to my room to go to sleep. The excitement and curiosity were burning inside like a little child opening gifts. I ripped the envelope open and was startled by all the small envelopes falling out.

Nine small envelopes were inside this BIG envelope, each from a different person showing interest in me.

The first letter read:

The Post
Lonely hearts

Hi, I'm a 22-year-old Indian male. On 23-26 February 1994, I came across the 'Lonely Hearts' column. I am interested in getting in contact with Miss Only Angel. I'm interested in meeting, writing, or talking to her over the phone. Anything will help in contacting her. Give her my address or my phone number.

Yours faithful
Ezekiel Maistry
27th February 1994

Each letter was so beautifully written, and I was always curious. I enjoyed reading every letter. It felt good when there were questions about me. I was incredibly moved. This experience was overwhelming as I was a timid and reserved person.

I knew about prayer, BUT I didn't know how to ask GOD for help regarding which of the eight to leave out.

What do I say, "*LORD, help me choose the right guy to continue to write to?* And so, I did just that.

I just said, *"GOD, which one shall I choose?"*

I then advised all nine guys that I could not correspond further due to my school demands. I didn't feel that bad; it was not like any of the nine guys, and I had met them face-to-face.

From all nine letters received, the very first letter I read on the first day was from **Ezekiel Maistry**. His replies were straightforward about his day, and he would ask me about mine. He is five years older than I am. By just reading his letters, I could sense his maturity.

After four months of writing to each other, I eventually decided to give in to his request to meet personally.

The much-awaited day, 21st May 1994, to meet him face to face, had arrived.

We recognised each other instantly.

Our date ended unexpectedly fast, with him walking me to the taxi rank. He waited until I was settled inside the taxi and left.

Mum was very serious about meeting Ezekiel before our relationship went any further.

While some couples wait months or even years before meeting each other's parents, we had done this first step in just **under a week**. This decision was a huge step.

Meeting our parents indicated that the couple was serious about each other.

I felt an anxiety attack taking over my body. Unfortunately, we had to abide by Mum's request if we wanted to move forward with the relationship. I did not even have time to meet him personally to prepare him for the meeting.

Meeting the Family for the First Time

Just the other Saturday, we introduced ourselves to each other, and ***a week later***, I introduced him to my family. It was as if there was a wedding taking place at home.

We sat and had lunch together; however, the day did not end *without* Ezekiel being told that he had to bring his parents over for the official introduction and that I was not allowed to go out of the house with him.

After that brief introduction, when Ezekiel was asked to bring his parents over, I knew that the formal introduction of our parents was a custom of initiating marriage.

My past was still playing a huge part in my life, and I didn't want this relationship to go any further without informing Ezekiel that this was my foster family, and for him to decide further.

However, the thought of telling him took me back to my childhood, leading to my teen years of hurt, and emotions started to resurface, which left me instinctively exposed to being injured and abandoned again.

Make Or Break Our Relationship

Despite my mind throwing warnings at me that he was going to reject me, just like my biological parents, I paid no heed to them. I knew I was following my heart; that was all that mattered. However, that didn't stop my aggressive thoughts from whispering,

"*The closer he drew to you, the faster he would run away after hearing your truth.*

The following Saturday, after lunch, we sat outside my house. I paused to think this through, knowing what I would reveal could make or break our relationship. "*I want you to know everything about me so that we can be real to each other,*" I said to Ezekiel.

I began to pour my heart out to him. I told the truth about being abandoned at the age of three by my biological mother, who was a prostitute and drug addict. I relayed the events that brought me to my foster family. I went on to explain that I had no idea who my biological family was.

Even though I felt the tears fill my eyes, it took all of me not to break down at that moment. After all, I had never cried in front of Ezekiel; this was only the third time seeing him, and chances were, if I started, I didn't think I could stop the flood of tears.

While I spoke, I saw his face, which was filled with empathy. He was calm and supportive and assured me he was not going anywhere. He held my hands, kissed my forehead, and held me for a while as we sat on the steps.

With so many emotions stirring, his reassurance allowed me to speak far more freely and openly than I thought I would have. I was comforted to see how well he was digesting all of this.

However, I knew that was not all I had to tell him. I had to tell him something that I had never shared with anyone, but fear gripped me so much that I cried very intensely. He thought I was crying because of what he had just heard. I eventually composed myself, wiped away my tears, and said to him, *"There is something else I want to share with you."* I almost wanted to avoid it and pretend there was nothing else, but this needed to be done.

His touch was warm as he caressed my back comfortingly, calming my heart. Ezekiel took my hand and caressed it supportively, encouraging me to talk. I didn't know what to feel about his affection.

"Due to my family's request to meet your parents immediately, it is evident that getting to know each other better before our families meet is not in our favour, but I can't hide such things from you.

You deserve to know everything before anything materialises between us, so you can decide whether you want to build a relationship with me or end it."

I took a deep breath and then continued. I felt nervous about exposing myself.

Father's Day

I went on to say that I hated Father's Day. It was a meaningless day for as long as I could remember. I emphasised that I didn't have a father figure in my life. I didn't know what it meant to have a lifelong love of a father, to be twirled around as his little girl, to sit in daddy's lap without it being a sexual thing.

I paused to compose myself. '*This is a huge risk you are taking,'* my deeper thoughts were saying as I glanced at Ezekiel's facial expression, which was filled with anger. I had heard that police officers are short-tempered.

Was this what 'short-tempered' looked like? I went on to narrate my story.

The truth was, I didn't know how to speak from my heart, for in the past, I wasn't supposed to.

"It started at a very young age," I continued.

"It happened when I was five years old. Something happened that I could not understand or explain, but somehow, I knew it was wrong. During the day, I would nap in the last room in the house.

Whilst sleeping on the bed, I would feel someone lifting my clothes from the bottom up. I would then feel a breeze between my legs. Not long after that, I would feel my panties being taken off and something touching my private part.

With my eyes closed, not understanding the gravity of what was going on, I would move from sleeping on my back or side to sleeping on my tummy, hoping it would stop, but it didn't; it just felt more and more painful and horrible.

"I would feel something going inside me between my legs, and this action would only stop when footsteps outside the room were heard, and then I would hear footsteps of someone walking away quickly and quietly.

*One day, I opened my eyes and saw the person who had removed my panties and caused me pain. I discovered that it was the person I called **'Dad.'***

*"As I got older, I understood that **Dad** was sticking his fingers inside my private part, which made me feel confused and bad about myself.*

This abuse went on for years. I recall in my teen years that on Wednesday nights, I would normally attend Bible studies with my mum, but due to school studies, on that particular Wednesday, I did not go.

After studying, I went to sleep. I can't remember why, but I slept on the floor; my brothers and dad were home. In my deep sleep, I felt something creeping up my legs. I clenched my thighs together, but despite my efforts, my underwear was pulled down.

"I felt the pressure of his penis against my vagina, and then

it entered my vagina. Even though I struggled to breathe, I screamed and found the strength to push him out of me. I firmly believe that it was the strength from GOD that I managed to push Dad off me.

That push prevented his penis from penetrating me fully. It was the night I will never forget, the night I escaped being raped. Whenever my dad crept up beside or behind me, I always found a way to wriggle myself out of that space."

I didn't want to sound revolting, but the disgust was evident in my voice. I couldn't stop crying. As much as I tried, the tears wouldn't stop falling. Ezekiel allowed me to cry without saying a single word. He held me as he rocked me back and forth.

He did not let go or try to create distance between us. I couldn't see Ezekiel's face; I didn't want to see his face, as I was unsure what he would say.

He muttered, *"It's okay,'* under his breath, but didn't let go of me. He hugged me tightly, reassuring me that everything would be okay.

'Well, he hasn't broken up with me yet. This could be a good sign, right?" I silently thought.

After a couple of minutes, I pulled my head away from his chest and wiped my tears away. I felt completely numb, and my mind went blank. I was unable to focus on anything.

"If you are going to break up with me, will you do it now, please?" I said with my heart, thumping at the thought of him breaking up with me.

'I'm not breaking up with you," Ezekiel interrupted me.

"But what if you regret this?" I asked.

"I won't," he reassured me.

"You have no idea how scared I was to lose you. I gave up on life long ago, but you brought me back. You filled my heart with desire; you made me feel the emotions I thought I had lost," I confessed.

"I'm not going to let this destroy us," he said firmly. His determined response resolved my emotional turmoil.

I paused and nearly broke down completely at his words. I tried to speak, but my lips trembled with every second.

It's a trauma that I've been struggling to live with for many years, I said while sobbing helplessly and incessantly. It was excruciating to recount all those details, but I had to tell the man I want to have and hold forever.

Social Worker

After I was told that I was not their biological daughter, it made sense why I had to accompany my parents from time to time to meet a lady in an office, whom I later learned was my Social Worker. I remember her asking my parents to leave the room while she chatted with me.

With the fear of Mum's words, '***Whatever happens in the house, stays in the house. You are not allowed to tell anyone our personal stuff.'*** I didn't tell her about the sexual abuse. I do regret not telling her.

Perhaps if I had, the abuse would have stopped, and it would have helped me understand these bad and mixed-up feelings I had experienced, but the fear of getting a hiding sealed my mouth.

I was a little hopeless girl who was clueless that her body had been abused.

When I came to understand that what my dad was doing was wrong, I was too ashamed, embarrassed, and confused to tell anyone. I lived every day, trying so hard to avoid being in the same room as him, but it became more and more difficult even under the same roof.

It seemed that as I grew up from a child to a teenager, his disgusting acts became more and more unbearable. I lived every day in fear, with the tormenting thought, *"Tonight is the night. He was going to rape me."*

I was destroyed physically, mentally, and emotionally, not to mention traumatised by the person who was supposed to protect and take care of me, **'Dad.'**

It was daunting having to disclose the sexual abuse to Ezekiel. Still, he was listening to my every word, which felt very strange because no one had given me that much attention, especially to listen to something as disgusting as this.

I went on to explain.

"I spent years battling to sleep. I was strongly attached to a special green blanket that I slept with. No matter how hot the weather was, and even though I got teased a lot for sleeping with a green woollen blanket during hot weather.

I would wrap the blanket around my legs so that when ***Dad*** *came to interfere with me late at night, I would be alarmed when he tried to remove the blanket. I was easily startled by any noises.*

To date, my family didn't understand, but being attached to this green blanket provided comfort and security throughout the night."

Peaceful Sleep

My grandmother was wonderfully warm. In her old age, she could hold herself with dignity and pride all her days. It was the only time when Granny shared a bed with me that I would sleep like a baby and know I was safe, safe from all the sexual abuse. There was no need for my green blanket. I wished she could stay with us forever.

Drained emotionally

I didn't have the emotional energy to speak, for I was breaking down emotionally while trying to explain everything. I didn't know what Ezekiel was going to do because, after all, he was a policeman.

Ezekiel interrupted my thoughts and expressed how upset and angry he was that I had brothers, yet no one could see what was happening underneath the roof.

Yes, the four brothers I grew up to admire, love, and look up to never came to rescue me.

The walls and the people who were supposed to keep me safe as a child didn't always. I continued to relate, saying that I would lie awake in bed every night and try to figure out how to stop him from entering my bed. These were the thoughts I lived with for years.

While pouring my heart to Ezekiel, I felt the brokenness hidden in my heart's deep recesses had been exposed.

Ezekiel assured me that now that he was in my life, he would not let my father ever come close to me with that evil intention. If he did, Ezekiel would personally take action to put an end to this disgusting action. For now, he would keep his cool and maintain his respect for the family, especially my father.

I knew that Ezekiel was GOD sent because, after introducing him to the family, the sexual abuse stopped.

What I thought would break my relationship with Ezekiel

strengthened it.

Our under-a-month relationship, from then on, became stronger each day.

Speaking up was scary, for it caused me immense amounts of anxiety, but it had also been empowering. Having Ezekiel to hear, believe in, and support me, I finally felt protected, safe, and loved.

Suddenly, life had a new meaning. Ezekiel was slowly invading my heart and taking his place there. It felt awesome to wake up suddenly knowing I was in love.

Indeed, Ezekiel was everything a woman could want and more.

A thousand words were not enough to say what I felt inside my newfound security. I enjoyed it when Ezekiel held my hands. Life was worth living. I was shaking and crying.

"There you have it; now you know everything. There are no more secrets,' I said with an expression that clearly showed that a great weight was finally lifted off me.

What started as a friendship had grown stronger. I didn't have the strength to show him. There had been so much heartache in my life, and I longed for the feeling of what love felt like.

Ezekiel made me realise that you do not love someone because they're perfect, but you love them, although they're not.

Was I growing powerfully attracted to him? Could it be that love had finally found me?

The **Love** I received from Ezekiel was unquestionable; it was instinctive and natural, making me feel complete.

In your misery, look at the positives.

Like you, I never chose to be so shattered, but somehow, through the agonising pieces of my wounds and brokenness, I managed to let GOD into my dark place.

Many people let their painful past consume, absorb, and hold them back. The past will and still has power over us, but we choose whether we live in the past or escape from it; it is your decision.

I have shared my darkest, most confidential, and most vulnerable experiences within these pages, from my imperfections to my ignorance of the outside world, to being mistreated, sexually abused, rejected, and abandoned. I want to challenge you to bring all the shattered pieces of your life, along with the scars from past wounds to GOD and let HIM do what only HE can do.

As I grew wiser and gained life experience, I reflected on my painful, rejected, and suffering journey. Knowing that Jesus will never leave or turn away from me means that I will never be alone for as long as HE is in my life, which made me smile through tears. Past wounds might still rage within you like an unforeseen storm, yet Christ brings peace amid enraged storms no matter how shattered we are.

To increase my confidence and self-esteem, I had to continuously shake off my routine of low self-esteem and leave my pity party. It exhausted me emotionally, but I was determined to rise above it. I would sometimes withdraw more and more. I knew I was supposed to impact the nation, even if it meant revealing my long-hidden past.

I often found anger more comfortable than fear. Anger gave me the sense of control while fear exposed my nakedness.

When I think of all the broken pieces of my life and in the lives of others that I had the honour and privilege of encountering, I know I was born for such a time as this, to bring healing through Jesus Christ.

The more damaged we feel on the inside, the more we want to keep our brokenness hidden from other people, so they won't judge us or laugh at us. I'm all too familiar with this feeling. No one saw the real me, even though I appeared to be there for everyone else.

You are probably in a state of depression, and life hasn't turned out like you thought it would. Would you still love a GOD you don't understand? When you allow what you came from to still cling to you, the question arises: *Do you want better?*

I've experienced bullying and teasing. I felt hurt and degraded. But I continued to trust GOD, and HE has given me hope. You will encounter those who wish to crush you throughout your life, but never forget that **GOD is on your side.**

My experiences have equipped me with love and the willingness to assist others in realising their potential.

A life of faith does not mean a life without pain, nor does a pain-filled life of faith mean a life without sunshine! I've discovered that when I put my everything into being strong. I easily forget about my weakness. We embrace the diverse qualities that make everyone unique.

Regardless of what you have been through, there is **beauty in your brokenness.** Believe that you have been chosen from your mother's womb to be a blessing to another.

My suffering served as a lesson, my loss as a present, my struggle as an opportunity, my success as a gift, my calling as comfort, and my life as a living testament. We all have a special story that shapes our personalities and characters, whether we are moms, fathers, daughters, or sons.

Perhaps you never reached your full potential because of the things you were derived from. I don't serve idols or statues. I serve a GOD who carries me, not me carrying Him, hence today by the grace, mercy, and strength of GOD, I stand in confidence. I'm not who I was before.

I discovered my victory sitting at HIS feet and in HIS hands. Remember, GOD sees you if no one saw your pain or looked at you with compassion. HE knows your every fear and what life did to you, but guess what, it didn't destroy you.

The purpose of CPR is to revive a person who is about to pass out. If people thought you were going to die, that you were not going to make it, they threw you away, said you would never get up, the devil is a liar. May you come out of isolation and come out of your excuses. I pray that you will allow GOD to resuscitate you to live again.

May this reading serve as a reminder that fulfilling your life's purpose depends on your relationship with Christ. Be kind and patient with yourself through whatever stage of awareness you are in.

Inspire before you expire.

Many people miss out on joy because they are too busy attempting to change other people's perceptions of themselves. Allowing ourselves to be joyful can make us feel vulnerable, but each time we give in to those feelings, we build resilience. When horrible things happen, we quietly grow stronger.

When you are ready to identify, confront, and conquer your past, you are prepared for GOD to heal, restore, and guide you to the destiny that He has for you. A destiny that goes beyond your expectations. GOD'S WORD can change your life and make it better.

The fact that you are reading this confirms that JESUS is reaching out to you with HIS love and kindness, full of forgiveness; embrace it, dear brother and sister.

WHO TOLD YOU that YOU are unworthy?

WHO TOLD YOU that YOU are unloved?

WHO TOLD YOU that YOU cannot shine?

WHO TOLD YOU that YOU are so messed up that GOD does not love you?

WHO TOLD YOU that it's too late, YOU can never accomplish anything?

WHO TOLD YOU that GOD won't use YOU for HIS Glory?

WHO TOLD YOU that YOU can't achieve anything in life or

can't be used to impact the nation?

If you're feeling unwanted, abandoned, or rejected, it's time to rejoice.

We have all experienced rejection. Whether it was from our childhood or later in life, we know the painful pangs of abandonment and hurt. The enemy desires to steal, kill, and destroy GOD's people, but it's time to gird ourselves with the sword of the Spirit and take back what the enemy attempted to steal from us. **Let us pray.**

May this prayer provide healing and restoration if you have been taken advantage of, abused, rejected, abandoned, or mistreated.

Lord, I am so thankful that You chose me. Even though the devil has tried to use people to tell me that I would never be worth anything, You wanted me and sought me out until I finally heard Your voice and surrendered to Your call.

I am so grateful that the world's opinion about me wasn't genuine. I'm happy that You pursued me with such a mighty love and refused to give up on me.

What else can I say to express my heart to You? I can only say, ***"Thank You, Jesus!"***

Look around you! See any seraphim? How about pearly gates? **NO?**

I don't see them either; there's a simple explanation. We are not at home YET. So, while you are still here on earth, you have been given a chance to live your God-given purpose.

My suffering served as a lesson, my loss as a present, my struggle as an opportunity, my success as a gift, my calling as comfort, and my life as a living testament. We all have a special story that shapes our personalities and characters, whether we are mothers, fathers, daughters, or sons.

For this reason, I want to support and motivate you to embrace and appreciate your imperfections so your loved ones can see your greatest version before you pass away! Don't give up; hold on.

This is my story, from being an orphan to having a difficult upbringing to becoming a woman overwhelmed with love.

Rox-Anne Maistry

- Blissfully married to Ezekiel since 30th November 1994.
- After facing challenges with three miscarriages, I'm grateful to be the proud MOTHER of two daughters: Ezel (22) and Rae-Anne (18).
- My husband and I were ordained as Pastors on 13th August 2012.
- **Who told you? Ministry**: Dealing with Inner Emotions.
- **KeNako** is a WhatsApp Prayer Group.
- **I'm blessed to be a blessing.** It is challenging for you to give on your birthday instead of receiving.
- **Pillow Talk**: If my pillow could talk, it would tell you of all my tears.
- **Breakthrough**: For the Unemployed.
- **AA** (Anointed and Appointed): You were anointed in my mother's womb and appointed as per GOD's perfect timing.
- **WINNER**: MRS. JOHANNESBURG PERSONALITY 2019.
- **Author of the Month**: March 2025 on America's Publisher.

My natural motto is *"action speaks louder than words,"* and my spiritual motto is *"empty hell...overpopulate HEAVEN."*

From Ruin to Radiance: the RESILIENT Heart

Coming back from a home of humble beginnings, my mum and dad are cousins. My granny and grandfather, who were brother and sister, arranged their wedding. My mum had no say in the matter. She was 19 when she had to get married. I have two siblings younger than me, my sister and brother. My dad worked as a waiter at a Country Club, and my mum stayed home and cared for us. The little that my dad earned did provide us well. He took good care of us. Children loved his funny character. We were lucky enough to have lived in a house provided by my dad's company.

Growing up, life would have been normal except that my dad had a drinking problem. He had access to alcohol due to where he worked. He would come home drunk, and there were times when he would abuse my mother physically, verbally, and emotionally. I remember a time when he dragged her out of the house in the middle of the night. Being the oldest, I always felt guilty that I couldn't do much to help my mum. My dad was a big man, and because of respect for our parents, we didn't get involved in their matters. Sometimes I was embarrassed to attend functions with my dad, hoping he wouldn't drink and create a scene, especially for school events like sports day and concerts. I never wanted my friends to see my dad being drunk.

My mum tried to leave my dad many times. I remember once when it was my matric year, and I couldn't attend some classes because Mum took my siblings and me to my granny's place. This time, she was sure to divorce Dad. She even got a lawyer, but my dad always brought her back. Although families knew about my father's drinking problem, no one helped. Instead, my uncles would entertain my dad with some drinks when we visited families for holidays. It was heartbreaking, especially seeing my mum so stressed. All I wanted was for my parents to be happy all the time.

The drinking never stopped, and neither did the beating of my mum. My sister tried to stop my dad once, and he had a knife and almost stabbed her. It haunts her to this day. I never knew how much anger, hurt, and bitterness she had carried all these years, until she recently exploded, pouring out to me all these feelings that held her captive. All these years, she couldn't move on, although now she has a family.

It's been 26 years since my dad passed away. I was upset with my dad for some time and blamed him for specific achievements I couldn't accomplish. The drinking affected me and my sister emotionally. My sister still has not forgiven my dad. My brother was too young to remember much. My mum is now 69 years old. She doesn't speak much about the abuse, but as strange as it might sound, she misses my dad. I might not understand her feelings; he was the one man she had known. She cared for him and also loved him. She still acknowledges his birthdays and death anniversary.

For me to move on, I tried to figure out what might have led my dad to behave in this way. I believe that at a very young age, he had his own struggles, having to leave school at a young age and work to support his family. While circumstances are not an excuse for his behaviour towards our family, I understand that because of his experiences, he turned to alcohol. I choose to see the good in him. While there were many challenging moments while we were growing up, there were also good moments. My parents still got along at times. Growing up, my parents, siblings, and I never said "I love you" to each other. And today I chose LOVE. I've FORGIVEN my father.

I'm sharing my story not to complain about my childhood but to help you stay hopeful and believe in yourself. Ask for help if you need it. Go for counselling, it is nothing to be ashamed of. Get help for your dad. There are so many resources available. Don't be scared to speak out. Don't carry this pain all your life. At some point, it will come crashing down on you like it did on my sister. To find peace and healing, you need to forgive to move on.

Many years ago, I didn't understand the plight of a widow in our family. I didn't know that she was screaming out her pain and frustrations in ways we couldn't understand. People judged her, including me, because I didn't understand. Thinking of my grandmothers and Mum, who were widowed at such early ages, were never allowed to mourn the loss of a husband. It was just family being around and taking charge of the rituals, but not much love and compassion were given to the widow herself. Nobody speaks about how exhausting grief can be. Life just went on as normal for them. The word widow was never mentioned. It was just expected for Grandma to be Grandma and Mum to be Mum. I always saw them as hard-working, tough ladies who had everything together. They were the most loving, caring people I know. They made grief look okay so that others won't fear it. They grieved in secret so as not to make anyone uncomfortable.

Every day, I wonder how many widows are quietly suffocating – showing up like they are okay when inside they are breaking. Today, I am walking on that path. I now know better; I understand it now. On the 16th of June 2021, I lost my husband to COVID-19. I never knew that there were so many emotions attached to a profound loss. You experience shock, numbness, sadness, isolation, anxiety, forgetfulness, worry, and fear. I could go on forever with this. It's like your life is perfect one day, and the next, it's shattered into a million pieces. Everything has been turned upside down, and you feel confused about your place in the world. You feel like you don't fit in anymore.

On the 14th of February 1998, I married my husband, Joshua Ray Solomon. We have two children, my 26-year-old son and my 22-year-old daughter. We have always been a very close-knit family. He was one of God's greatest gifts to me, and I'll always be thankful for our love and life. He was a man who showed me a different side to life. He had his priorities straight with God at the centre, me, family, work–it went in that order.

He was wise yet humble, a faithful man. He worked hard, loved hard, and prayed hard. No matter how much I nagged him, he never raised his voice at me. He spoke respectfully. He was a great father. And yes, there were times when we had disagreements, but we always tried to sort it out before the end of the day. We prayed together. Had our family devotions. He loved making jokes and doing funny things. His laugh was infectious. He listened to decent music and sang very well. Everyone loved him. He was one in a million and was once in a lifetime for me.

I am incredibly thankful to have known such love in this life. He was the best man I have ever known, and I spent 23 years by his side. I wish I could say I never took the time we had together for granted, but today I look back over the messy, beautiful life we shared, and I'm thankful for every moment. Even the hard times. Perhaps, especially in the challenging moments. For it was in those moments that he taught me the most about God.

We went through a lot of challenges along the way. I was held up at gunpoint at work and had my wedding ring, mobile phone, and cash taken, and then I was hit on my head with the gun. When I called on the name of Jesus, it disturbed the robber, he then pointed the gun at me and said, *"What Jesus?! What Jesus?!"* I just said, "*Lord, my life is in your hands,*" and he slowly put the gun down and left.

I usually fetch my son after school and bring my husband to work. My son was six at the time. On that day, I completely forgot to pick him up. A friend called me earlier to say my son was safe with her, and I could pick him up after work. I hate to think what would have happened if he had not been there. I believe that God had protected him. However, the experience did leave me traumatised for a while. I couldn't walk in public places because every face I saw looked like them. I had nightmares. And slowly began to heal.

A month later, our house was broken into and all our jewellery, some of which had sentimental worth, camera, cash, etc, whatever the robbers could carry was gone as they gained entrance from a small window. In 2010, while everyone was enjoying the football World Cup, we discovered that our house and car were being repossessed, and we couldn't do anything to save them. It was too late; we only had two weeks to move out of the house. We cried out to God to please make a way for us. "Help us, Lord, we can't lose our home, where would we go?"

What about our children? Why is this happening to us? I couldn't understand God's plan for us. It seemed like God was silent. But we couldn't give up on Him. Not long after, Ray was offered his retrenchment package at work. After careful consideration, he accepted the offer, seeing a way out to settle all our debts, which meant sacrificing 27 years of service to his company. This decision also meant he would be out of a job.

Ray was offered a six-month renewable contract job in another province, eleven hours from home. That meant we would only be seeing him once a month. Being a contract position, the children and I couldn't move in with him. This arrangement went on for four years, until Ray got a letter saying his contract was coming to an end. We were excited that he was coming home and could once again be together as a family.

Two weeks before his contract had ended, Ray came home. That weekend, we enjoyed spending time with him. His presence always lit up the house. He would do funny things just to make us laugh. We spoke and made plans that by the end of the month, the children and I would go with him and help him pack and drive back together. That night, we had our family devotion. Ray told the children to trust God even in their lowest. He spoke of how God always came through for him, no matter his challenges. He said he was not even qualified for his job, but God had a reason for placing him there. We then prayed as a family.

A couple of days later, Ray went back to his workplace. Then he called to say he had tested positive for COVID-19. I made the eleven-hour journey to be with him. The next day, Ray complained of chest pains and was admitted to the hospital. Once he was admitted, he called to say he was feeling so much better. I was not allowed to visit him because of the "NO VISITORS" rule due to the COVID-19 restrictions.

He seemed to be getting better the first two days in the hospital. He sounded so much better. I hoped he would be discharged so he'd make it home in time to celebrate Father's Day with the children in a week. But on the third day, I got a call from the doctor saying my husband's lungs were weakening and they didn't have enough ventilators, and he would be airlifted the next morning to a hospital near the home where we lived.

That evening, I made arrangements to go back home, but first decided to stop at the hospital. I entered the hospital and asked the receptionist if I could see my husband. She said visitors are not allowed. I started to cry. I just wanted to see my husband. The receptionist then called for the doctor. I asked the doctor if I could see my husband. She was very kind and said she would try to arrange for me to see my husband, even for just five minutes. I felt a huge relief. She then took me through the back entrance and made me wear complete Personal Protective Equipment (PPE).

I entered the room where my husband was. There were three other patients there as well. The doctor warned me not to go near him, so I stood by his bedside. He was sleeping, and the nurse woke him up. As soon as he saw me, his face lit up and he said, “You came.” I said I had to see him because I missed him. He thought I would go with him to the hospital where he would be transferred, but the doctor quickly replied that she couldn't come.

I wished I could have hugged him or just held his hand. I got to speak to him for just a little while. I told him he needed to stay strong, that we would get through this, and that everyone was praying for him. I assured him that he would be coming home soon. And then it was time to leave. I said my farewell, “I love you,” and he said, “I love you too.” I didn't want to leave him alone. Holding back the tears in my eyes, I started walking towards the door, and he called my name, “Verush.” When I turned back, he threw a kiss and said, “I love you,” again. And I also did the same, not knowing that this would be the last time I was going to see my husband alive.

The next day, I received the dreaded phone call. “Your husband has left us.” I couldn't grasp what was being said. Left where?! Was he airlifted to the other hospital? I asked again where my husband was. “I'm sorry, Ma'am, but your husband is not with us anymore. He passed away at 10:45 A.M.” I was numb. I couldn't speak. Did I hear right? My husband, my best friend, my other half is gone. It couldn't be true. I felt shocked to the core. I tried calling his phone, hoping he would answer and that this was all a bad dream.

I thought I had already faced the worst throughout my life. I'd been through hard things that tested, stretched, and knocked me down. But I made it through. God has seen me through, and I always had my husband with me as we faced these many challenges together. The many material possessions we lost were replaced (the house, car, jewellery, etc). Everything that I lost was replaced. But Ray could NEVER be replaced.

I never expected to become a widow at 45. I still needed Ray and felt he had much more to live for. Now I am left to face the heartache of grief alone. It was difficult not to hear Ray's voice again. I expected the phone to ring and for him to suddenly walk through the door. It still felt like Ray was working away from home. People tried to say things in the hope that it would comfort me. But it made no sense to me, especially when they said, *"At least he's in a better place."* All I could think was I wish he was still here. I tried to hide my emotions. I didn't want people to feel sorry for me. I pretended to be okay. Most times, I felt like I didn't fit in. I could be in a crowd and still feel alone.

I couldn't understand why God was allowing me to feel so much pain. I cried to Him; my prayers were more complaints to Him than praises. I would force myself to go to church, knowing how involved my husband was in the church. He played the drums, sometimes the guitar, and led worship. I didn't feel strong. I just had faith the size of a mustard seed. Even that was slipping. But then God came through. He restored and reminded me who He is.

Apart from mourning and the shock of losing my husband, there are so many other things to deal with, from not having any bills to pay to sorting out everything on my own and doing all the legal paperwork. I didn't have a clue where to begin. My husband always wanted to explain what to do should anything happen to him, but I always stopped that conversation. I didn't want to speak about death. We always thought we would have more time. But it is one of the most important discussions with your spouse. You will be more clued up on what to do.

It was so hard for me to console my children. I was feeling so helpless and lost myself, I didn't want them to see me crying all the time. As much as I tried being strong, they did the same for me. I know how much they miss their dad. Life as we knew it ended when my husband died. We are making strides every day to do what my husband has taught us, to press on. To seek the Lord. To continue his work. To leave a legacy of faithfulness and to never lose our sense of humour. Death anniversaries, birthdays, and special days are hard. It was bittersweet moments for me when my children succeeded in their careers. We always try to include him by taking a family photo with a picture frame of my husband.

It's been four years into widowhood, and people think my grief is gone because I can function. One doesn't get over grief; one works around it. Today, I am doing much better than I had ever imagined possible. I attribute this to the incredible grace, wisdom, and comfort God gave me through His word and the support of my family, the church, and the amazing people He sent me.

I have joined a widow's support group called White Flowers, and seeing how much I could relate to these ladies gave me an idea to start a widow's support group in my community.

I started the Widows Circle of Strength support group in January 2025. I have so much love and respect for these brave and inspiring women. Only when you lose a loved one will you truly understand the strength it takes to move forward. Life as a widow can be full of grief, pain, and loneliness. But through this, we also find strength, courage, and independence. We grieve with hope and faith. In creating this group, I have made a community of people who understand everything we have all been through. We have bonded over our losses, and we have built friendships.

The beauty and hard thing about suffering is that it leaves a person stripped of everything but Jesus. As much as I desire God to restore all I've lost, I've found that true healing only comes when I crave God's presence more than anything else. Is God still good even in this? There are so many things I don't know. There are so many questions to which I wish I had the answers, but I know this one thing: God is good all the time. As my journey as a widow continues, I am grieving with hope and leaning on Jesus.

Verushka Solomon

Verushka Solomon is a newly published co-author whose heartfelt storytelling is rooted in deep personal experience, resilience, and a calling to uplift others. Born on 26 August 1975 in South Africa, Verushka is the eldest of three siblings. She was blessed with a beautiful 23-year marriage to her late husband, Joshua Ray Solomon, until his passing four years ago. Together, they built a loving family and raised two remarkable children, Delano and Raecal.

Currently based in the small town of Mandeni, Verushka works as an administrative clerk and has built a career across diverse sectors, including construction, transport, and the fuel industry. But beyond her professional background lies a deeper purpose: using her pain as a platform to bring healing and hope to others.

After becoming a widow, Verushka recognised a gap in emotional support for women who had experienced similar loss. In response, she founded a widows' support group in her community—a safe space where women gather to share stories, encourage one another, and walk the healing path together. Her lived experience has transformed her into a beacon of compassion and a catalyst for change.

Through her debut as a co-author, Verushka amplifies her message of faith, courage, and new beginnings. She is passionate about helping others transition from seasons of grief to renewed purpose, and her story continues to inspire readers worldwide.

Hope is Worth Protecting Because Light is Better Than Darkness

This chapter is dedicated to all who have walked through the valleys of trauma, faced the storms of pain, and encountered the many challenges that life can bring. To those who have felt broken, weary, or uncertain, these pages offer hope, encouragement, and the reminder that you are never alone on your journey. I especially dedicate this work to my mother, Mrs Agnes Cecilia Micah-Orgen, whose unwavering courage, faith, and love have guided me through every storm. Her resilience and wisdom have shaped the person I am today, and her example continues to inspire me to live with integrity, strength, and compassion.

I also dedicate this chapter to my beloved wife, Mrs Sarah Orgen, whose partnership, encouragement, and steadfast belief in me have made every challenge lighter and every triumph sweeter. Her love and support are a daily reminder of the power of unity, patience, and hope. My daily inspiration is our children, David Sam, Daniel Albert, and Deborah Grace Orgen. Your laughter, curiosity, and innocence remind me of the beauty of life and the importance of leaving a legacy of love, purpose, and faith. May this chapter serve as a reflection of my journey and a testimony of the hope, courage, and resilience that your generation can carry forward.

Finally, this work is dedicated to all who dare to dream, to rise after falling, and to keep walking forward even when the path seems uncertain. May it serve as a light to guide your steps, a source of comfort in difficult times, and a call to embrace life with hope, purpose, and unshakable faith.

Introduction

Sometimes, the world becomes so noisy and chaotic that we forget what truly matters. The constant rush of information, the endless demands of life, and the weight of uncertainty can overwhelm, and hope feels almost out of reach. Yet even in the most challenging moments, even when all seems lost, a single spark of hope can ignite a wave of change, lighting the path forward for ourselves and others. We are living in such a time. Around us, we see the consequences of conflict, broken communities, struggling families, and uncertain futures. The news often reminds us of despair and hardship, and it can be tempting to feel powerless. And yet, even amid all this, some stories shine like stars in the night, stories of courage, resilience, kindness, and unity that refuse to be dimmed. These stories matter. They deserve to be heard. They can change lives, restore faith, and ignite action.

Beacon of Hope: A Catalyst for Change is more than a book. It is a mission, a call to witness, and a call to action. It brings together voices from people who have faced profound challenges and consciously decided to respond with love, leadership, and vision. It is written for the mother who rebuilt her life after loss, finding strength she did not know she had; for the young person who rose to stand for justice, even when the world told them to stay silent; for the teacher who inspired a struggling student to believe in themselves; and for the leader who persevered despite overwhelming odds. These stories remind us that hope is not passive but active, courageous, and contagious.

And your voice matters, too. Whether you are a dreamer who sees beauty where others see brokenness, a survivor whose strength inspires those around you, or someone who quietly but faithfully takes action to make the world better, your story has the potential to make a difference. Every word you share could offer hope to someone feeling lost. Every insight you offer could spark a shift in a heart, a family, or a community. Every truth you speak could inspire change far beyond your immediate reach.

Hope is real. It is not only a feeling but a choice, a force, and a responsibility that we all share. When voices come together in pursuit of goodness, no darkness is too strong, no challenge too great, and no barrier too high. The power of collective hope can transform communities, mend broken hearts, and lead generations toward light. If you have ever wanted your life to make a difference beyond your own time, this is your moment. The opportunity to be a catalyst, a spark, and a beacon is here.

Let us rise together. Let us speak the truth boldly. Let us act with courage, integrity, and compassion. Let us create a light that shines across borders, gives courage to the weary, and guides countless others toward a brighter, more hopeful tomorrow. Our voices, stories, and actions can become the change we wish to see. Let this book be a starting point. Let it inspire you to be more than a witness, to hope to be a carrier of it.

The Power of One Light

A single candle in a dark room changes everything. Its flame may be small, but it immediately transforms the space. Shadows retreat, even if only a little. The darkness does not disappear entirely, but the atmosphere shifts. The eye begins to see again. The heart starts to hope again. The light reminds us that shadows have limits, and that light always holds the final word, even in the deepest darkness. The same is true in life. One small act of kindness can transform the heaviest day for someone who feels lost or invisible. A single message of encouragement, sent at the right moment, can keep a person from giving up entirely. A conversation over a cup of tea, a listening ear, or a warm smile can remind a grieving soul that they are seen, loved, and not alone.

We often imagine that change requires vast resources, large movements, or powerful titles. We may think our actions are too small, our words too quiet, or our efforts too insignificant. And yet, if we look closely at history, the most significant movements often began with one person who refused to let the darkness be the only story told. One voice, one choice, one small act of courage, this is how revolutions begin.

Consider the woman secretly giving food to a hungry child when no one was watching. Consider the teacher who spent extra hours helping a struggling student understand a lesson. Consider the neighbour who offered a simple prayer, a warm meal, or a helping hand. These small acts, these quiet lights, have ripple effects far beyond what the eye can see. Here is the truth: you can be that one person. You do not have to wait for the "perfect" time or the "right" opportunity. Every day presents countless moments where your words, presence, or actions can ignite a spark in someone's world. A compliment, a smile, a moment of patience, or a decision to stand for what is right, all of these are candles in the darkness.

Never underestimate the quiet courage it takes to be a light. It may not make headlines. It may not be celebrated on social media. But it matters. It changes hearts, restores hope, and can even change the course of someone's life. One small light can spark many more. One act of love can inspire countless others to do the same. So today, remember this: the world needs your light, not in grand gestures alone, but in the everyday choices where you decide to shine. Your presence, your words, your love, your courage, they are all beacons. They remind others that the darkness is not endless, that hope is real, and that even the smallest flame can make a difference. You can be the one to shift the atmosphere. You can be the one to bring warmth where it is cold, clarity where it is confused, and courage where it has faded. Light has a way of multiplying, and the world needs your light now more than ever. Step forward, shine brightly, and trust that even the smallest candle can hold back the night.

Ordinary People, Extraordinary Impact

The world's most powerful transformations rarely come from the famous, the wealthy, or those with grand titles alone. Actual change often begins with ordinary people who simply choose to act, refuse to look away, and believe that even their small corner of the world matters. Think of the farmer who shares his last seeds with a neighbour after a drought destroys the crops. He has nothing left for himself, yet he gives, trusting that a single act of generosity can spark renewal. Think of the young woman who tutors children under a single flickering streetlamp because the school has no electricity. Her hands are tired, her voice hoarse, but she refuses to let darkness steal the children's chance to learn. Think of the retiree who converts her garage into a food pantry because she noticed her neighbours going hungry. She does it quietly, without recognition, simply because she cannot ignore the need before her eyes.

None of these people was waiting for applause. They were not seeking fame or recognition. They simply responded to the needs right before them, choosing courage over comfort and action over inaction. And in doing so, they created ripples that spread far beyond their immediate reach. Hope works the same way; it is contagious. One person's faithfulness inspires another to act. One person's courage allows others to be brave. One person's kindness reminds another that the world is not as cold as it sometimes seems. Your contribution may feel small at the moment, almost invisible. But when it joins with the efforts of others, it becomes part of something far greater that can change the course of a family, transform a street, uplift a school, and even influence the future of a nation.

Consider history itself. Many individuals whose names fill textbooks were once ordinary people, showing up day after day, quietly doing what was right. Their extraordinary impact was born not from privilege, but from persistence, faith, and the courage to care. The seamstress who stitched uniforms for soldiers, the teacher who stayed late to help struggling students, the neighbour who opened their home to those in need, these are the ones who often go unnoticed, yet whose contributions shape generations. The truth is simple: ordinary people who keep showing up, doing what is right, and refusing to give in to despair are often the extraordinary ones in history. They remind us that impact is not measured by fame or fortune, but by faithfulness, love, and the willingness to act.

So, when you think your efforts are too small or believe your actions won't matter, remember this: every kind word, selfless deed, moment of courage is a spark. And when sparks meet, they can ignite a fire that transforms the world. You need not be famous, wealthy, or powerful to make a difference. You only need to show up, act with love, and trust that your ordinary life can create extraordinary change.

The Courage to Begin

Fear is a constant companion in every journey toward change. It whispers in quiet moments: "What if you fail?" "What if no one listens?" "What if you are not enough?" Fear tries to hold hope back, telling us that our dreams are too big, our actions too small, and our voices too quiet. Yet courage is not the absence of fear; it is moving forward even when fear is still in the room. It is taking the next step, even when doubt presses against your heart. You do not need to have the entire plan perfectly mapped out before you start. You do not need ideal conditions, unlimited resources, or complete certainty. You simply need to begin where you are, use what you have, and do what you can. The smallest first step, taken in faith, can grow into something far greater than you imagine.

History is full of examples of humble beginnings that became extraordinary movements. Letters written at kitchen tables changed the course of nations. Conversations held in small living rooms sparked revolutions of thought and action. Ideas shared over simple cups of tea became the foundations for education, community, and hope. I am reminded of a young man in South Sudan, who began teaching children to read under the shade of a tree because the nearest school had been destroyed by conflict. He had no books, no formal classroom, only a stick to write letters and numbers in the dirt. And yet, he began. His courage inspired others, and today that humble gathering has grown into a full school with hundreds of students, a place of learning, hope, and opportunity. All of this began because he was willing to take the first imperfect step.

The truth is that beginnings have a special kind of power. They gather momentum in ways we often cannot see. One small step forward can inspire another person to take their own step. One act of courage can draw in others who were waiting for someone to lead the way. No matter how modest, each effort has the potential to multiply, creating a wave of change that touches countless lives. So, do not wait for perfection. Do not wait for permission. Do not wait for fear to leave the room entirely. Begin. Start with what you can do today. Speak the word, lend a hand, share your knowledge, extend kindness, or simply show up. Every beginning carries within it the seed of transformation. Every step taken in faith is a step that others can follow. And together, these steps have the power to change families, communities, nations, and even the world. Courage is contagious. Momentum attracts momentum. And hope, once it begins, is unstoppable. The only requirement is that you take the first step.

Stories That Heal

Our stories are more than memories tucked away in photo albums or journals. They are living testimonies, powerful vessels carrying the experiences, lessons, and resilience we have gained along life's journey. Each story can heal wounds that cannot be seen, awaken courage we did not know we possessed, and spark hope in lost hearts.

When we share the story of overcoming an illness, we do more than offer hope. We provide a roadmap for someone else walking the same path, showing them that recovery, growth, and joy are possible. When we speak about rebuilding after loss, heartbreak, or failure, we let others imagine life beyond their own ruins. Our journeys, no matter how ordinary they seem, can illuminate a path for someone still finding their way.

I remember meeting a man in Spain who had battled severe depression for more than a decade. He suffered in silence for years, believing that no one could understand. Finally, he chose to share his journey at a small community gathering. Afterwards, people came forward one by one to thank him, not because he had all the answers or solutions, but because his honesty helped them feel less alone. His story had pierced the veil of isolation and fear, creating connection and hope where there had been only darkness. The beauty of storytelling is that it reaches places statistics cannot. Numbers can describe a problem, charts can illustrate trends, but only a story can touch a heart. A well-told truth lingers, echoing long after data has been forgotten. Your story matters, despite how small or ordinary it may seem. Someone, somewhere, is struggling with the same fear, the same pain, or the same question that you have already faced. Your voice may be the rope they need to climb out of despair.

Think of each story shared as a lighthouse on a stormy coast. Ships in the night—tired, battered, and unsure—see the light and realise they are not lost. Every testimony of courage, resilience, and hope reminds others that they are seen and understood, and that survival is possible. In telling our stories, we build bridges of empathy, understanding, and love. Remember that your story could be someone else's lifeline, even when it feels uncomfortable or vulnerable to share. Each story is a seed planted in the heart of another, a spark that can grow into courage, faith, and change. Sharing offers hope, a declaration that no one has to face life's battles alone.

In Beacon of Hope, every story matters. Every voice matters. Every lived experience has the potential to heal, to inspire, and to guide others through the darkness. The light you shine through your story may reach farther than you can imagine, touching lives, lifting spirits, and reminding the world that hope is always possible—even amid the storm.

Unity in Action

Hope is powerful in one person, but when it is shared, it becomes unstoppable. One heart filled with courage can inspire others, but a community united in purpose can accomplish what no single person could achieve alone. When people come together, bound by compassion, shared values, and a desire to help, even the greatest challenges can be met with resilience and creativity. Unity does not always appear in grand gestures or massive projects. Sometimes it is quiet, humble, and practical. It is seen in neighbours who decide to repaint a worn-out playground, so children have a safe place to play, rather than waiting for the city to act. It is found in shop owners who agree to keep their lights on late during blackouts, creating a sense of security in their streets. It is visible in the willingness to lift others, share what you have, and put the community's needs above personal comfort.

I remember visiting a small town in the Philippines after a devastating flood. Homes were damaged, electricity was out for weeks, and despair hung heavily over the streets. But the residents did not wait for trucks or official instructions. They acted together. Some cooked meals for those who had lost their kitchens. Others organised childcare so parents could focus on rebuilding their homes. Local carpenters volunteered their time and skills to repair houses, and neighbours who had little of themselves shared what they could. One man said, “We didn’t need to be told what to do. We knew we had each other, and that was enough to start.” Their unity became a force of restoration, hope, and resilience.

A mission like Beacon of Hope thrives in this same spirit. We do not have to agree on everything to stand together. We do not need perfection, total harmony, or uniform beliefs to create change. We need to agree that light is better than darkness, that compassion is stronger than indifference, and that hope is worth protecting. When communities act together, ordinary people become extraordinary agents of change. Small actions accumulate, and a culture of care and courage spreads far beyond what anyone could accomplish alone.

Unity also teaches us that our differences are not weaknesses but opportunities. Each person brings unique talents, perspectives, and gifts. When combined with a shared commitment to a higher purpose, they multiply the impact of every effort. When joined with others, one person’s skills can repair homes, feed families, educate children, and lift spirits in ways that a single person could never manage. In today’s world, where division often dominates headlines, unity in action is revolutionary. Standing together, helping one another, and committing to collective hope is more than a strategy; it is a statement of faith. It says: We see the light. We will protect it. We will carry it forward together. So, let us take inspiration from those who have lived it. Remember that unity is more than agreement; it is action, service, and shared commitment. Let us choose to come together, to combine our strengths, and to shine light into every corner where darkness threatens. When hope is multiplied through community, it becomes unstoppable, and the world itself begins to change—one small act at a time, one life at a time, one community at a time.

Choosing Hope in Hard Seasons

Hope is easy to hold when skies are clear, and the sun warms your face. It flows naturally when life feels simple, and the path ahead is bright. But true hope is tested when storm clouds gather, when loss hits hard, when grief feels endless, and the road ahead seems impossible. In these moments, hope is not a gift but a choice. It is something you fight for, nurture, and protect, even when it feels as though the world is determined to steal it from you.

I remember meeting a mother named Angela in 2016. She had lost her only child to illness, a loss so deep that for months she couldn't find the strength to leave her bed. Every day, she felt grey, heavy, and hopeless. Yet one morning, something small stirred inside her, a decision to plant flowers in her front yard just to see something grow again. That simple act became a daily ritual, a tiny rebellion against despair. As the flowers bloomed, neighbours stopped to admire them, asking questions, and smiling again. Soon, Angela was giving away seeds, teaching others how to plant, and encouraging her community to create colour and life where there had been only sadness. Years later, her small act of defiance against grief has transformed the entire street, a living testament that hope can grow even in the hardest seasons.

Choosing hope does not mean pretending that everything is fine. It does not mean ignoring pain, loss, or disappointment. Choosing hope means looking honestly at the challenges before you and declaring, "This is not the end of the story." It means planting flowers when the soil is dry, speaking encouragement when voices are heavy with sorrow, and taking one step forward when the weight of the world seems too much to bear. Some days, choosing to hope requires extraordinary courage. Other days, it is a quiet and small deep breath, a prayer, a simple act of kindness. Whenever you choose hope, you strengthen the muscle that carries you forward.

The truth is that hope is contagious. When one person chooses to rise, even in despair, it allows others to rise. When one life refuses to surrender to darkness, it lights the way for countless others. Hard seasons are unavoidable, but hope is always available. It's the seed in the soil, the candle in the night, the hand that reaches out when others are falling. Your hope matters not just for you, but for the people around you. Choosing to hope creates a ripple that spreads beyond what the eye can see. It transforms grief into resilience, loss into purpose, and despair into action. Whenever you choose hope, you declare that life, love, and light are stronger than pain, fear, and darkness. So, in your own hard seasons, remember Angela and the flowers she planted. Remember that even the smallest act of courage and hope can bloom into something greater than you imagined. Keep choosing to hope, day after day, moment by moment. Each choice is a victory, each act a seed, and each day a step toward brighter tomorrows.

The Responsibility of Light

If you have been given light through wisdom, experience, resources, kindness, or healing, you carry a responsibility to share it. Light is not meant to be hidden, hoarded, or kept for ourselves. It is intended to illuminate paths, warm hearts, and guide others through the darkness. When we keep our light to ourselves, the world loses the brilliance that could transform lives. I remember meeting a man named Lwazi in Cape Town. He had survived a brutal attack that left him with lasting injuries, both visible and invisible. Many would have expected him to retreat from the world, to protect himself and withdraw into silence. But Lwazi chose differently. He began mentoring young men in his neighbourhood, teaching them practical skills like job training and the harder lessons of conflict resolution, emotional control, and hope. “I know what it’s like to live in the shadows,” he told me. “If I have even a match’s worth of light, I will use it.” His courage and commitment turned his suffering into a beacon for others, showing that one person’s light, when shared, can ignite countless others.

Your light is never just for you. It belongs to your family, community, city, and generation. It belongs to anyone wandering in darkness and searching for a guide. Think of the teacher who spends extra hours helping students understand difficult lessons, the neighbour who opens their door to someone in need, the professional who shares knowledge to empower others, or the friend who listens patiently when someone struggles with grief or doubt. Each act, however small, is a light being shared. The greatest tragedy is not that darkness exists; it always will. Shadows will fall, storms will rage, and challenges will appear. The tragedy is when those carrying light hide it out of fear, insecurity, or selfishness. Even the tiniest flame has the power to guide someone through the night. A single candle can show the way out of a dark room. A kind word can bring clarity to a confused mind. A shared story of resilience can remind someone that survival, healing, and joy are possible.

Carrying light is a responsibility, but it is also a privilege. Every act of sharing, every moment of courage, and every demonstration of kindness multiplies the impact of that light. You do not need all the answers, complete resources, or perfect circumstances. You only need to step forward and be willing to offer what you have. Your experience, wisdom, compassion, and courage are powerful tools enough to spark hope and transformation wherever they are shared. So, ask yourself: How can I let my light shine today? Who is waiting for a glimmer of guidance, a spark of encouragement, or a hand of support? Every choice to share what we have is a decision to push back darkness and create space for hope. Remember, the smallest flame can pierce the deepest shadow. Your light matters—not just for your journey, but for the countless lives it touches along the way.

Your Voice, Your Legacy

We live in a world obsessed with speed, instant results, and immediate recognition. Social media, fast-moving news, and the pressure for quick success make us feel that only what is visible today matters. Yet real, lasting change rarely happens overnight. Some of the most profound transformations in history unfolded slowly, quietly, over the years, even decades. That is why legacy matters. Legacy is not about monuments, titles, or the crowd's applause. It is about the seeds we plant today, small acts of faith, courage, and kindness that will bear fruit long after we are gone. Legacy is in the child you mentor who goes on to mentor others. It is in the community you help heal, which will stand stronger and more united for the generations to come. It is in the values you live out consistently, inspiring those who watch you to follow in your footsteps.

I once visited the Philippians and met an elderly man who had devoted his lifetime to planting trees along a barren hillside. He had planted over 1,000 trees, patiently nurturing each sapling for decades. Today, those trees provide shade for weary travellers, prevent soil erosion, and serve as homes for birds. When asked why he had begun such a monumental task, he simply said, "I wanted my grandchildren to walk in a forest, not a desert." His legacy was not built for recognition, but for the future, an enduring gift for those who would come after him.

Your legacy can take many forms. Perhaps it is kindness, small, consistent acts that remind others they are seen and valued. It may be courage, speaking truth, standing for justice, or taking risks that inspire others to do the same. It may be generosity, wisdom, or service, quietly shaping the world in ways that are invisible today but monumental tomorrow.

Whatever form it takes, plant it intentionally. Nurture it. Protect it. Live it. Think of your actions as seeds scattered in fertile soil. Some will grow quickly. Others may take years to sprout. Some will blossom after you have gone. That is the beauty of legacy: it transcends our own lifespan and becomes part of the ongoing story of humanity. Someone will rest in the shade of the trees you planted, learn from the lessons you shared, or feel courage because you dare to act when others hesitate. Your voice matters. Your choices matter. Your life matters, not only for today, but for the countless tomorrows your influence touches. Every word spoken, every hand extended, every life impact contributes to the story of your legacy. And while you cannot control every outcome, you can choose how you live today, knowing that the seeds you plant now have the potential to grow into forests of hope, resilience, and light for generations yet to come. So, as you move forward, remember this truth: your voice carries power, your actions carry meaning, and your life carries a legacy. Plant wisely, act courageously, and love generously. The world will feel the impact of your choices long after today has passed.

When the Road Feels Long

There will be seasons when hope feels like carrying a heavy lantern up a steep hill, slow, exhausting, and sometimes lonely. The weight of responsibility, the unending challenges, and the insurmountable setbacks can make it tempting to pause, to question whether the effort is worth it. In those moments, the journey feels longer than your strength, and the light you carry may seem dim. But remember this: light often travels farther than we can see. The impact of your actions may quietly unfold in places you will never visit, in hearts you will never meet, and in lives you will never fully understand. Every act of kindness, every word of encouragement, every courageous choice has a ripple effect. It moves through time and space in ways invisible to the eye but powerful in effect.

I recall meeting a nurse in a refugee camp in Canada. Day after day, she worked twelve-hour shifts tending to the injured and the sick. She often questioned whether her efforts made any difference. The needs seemed endless, and the exhaustion overwhelming. Then, months later, a young boy she had cared for returned, walking on his own for the first time. In his hand, he carried a drawing of a sunrise, a simple thank you that touched her heart. That moment reminded her that even the quietest acts can create ripples of hope that travel far beyond what we can measure. Hope is not a sprint. It is a marathon, sometimes a relay. There will be days when you carry the baton alone, and sometimes it lasts before you can pass it to another. What matters is that the flame keeps moving forward. Even when the climb is steep, the path is uncertain, the light you carry can guide others, inspire courage, and heal brokenness.

The world does not need perfect heroes. It needs people willing to act, share what they have, and persist when the road feels long. It needs voices willing to speak truth, hands willing to serve, and hearts willing to love, even when it is hard. And here is the most essential truth: the moment you decide to share your light, your voice becomes a beacon of hope to others. Your courage, kindness, and story will inspire someone you may never meet. The smallest act can grow into something extraordinary, changing lives in ways you may never fully witness. So, carry your lantern steadily. Step forward with faith, even when the path is steep. Speak, act, and love with intention, knowing that your life is part of a larger story of hope, resilience, and transformation. The road may feel long, but every step matters. Every word matters. Every choice matters.

And when you continue to shine, even in the darkest seasons, you help light the way for countless others, leaving a legacy far beyond your journey. This is your call. This is your moment. Step forward. Shine brightly. And let the world feel the light that only you can give.

Carry the Light Forward

As I bring this chapter to a close, I want to speak directly to you, the reader. You are not here by accident. You picked up this book because something deep within your heart knows that hope matters, your story matters, and your life carries the power to make a difference. Every chapter you've read, every story of courage, resilience, and unwavering faith, carries a single, undeniable message: light matters, and it grows only when it is shared.

Life will not always be easy. Storms will come. Unexpected losses, setbacks, and periods of uncertainty will test your faith, patience, and resolve. There will be moments when the climb feels steep, the path seems endless, and the world's troubles threaten to overwhelm you. Yet even in those moments, you carry a spark that can ignite hope, courage, and change far beyond what you can see. A single act of kindness, a smile to a stranger, a word of encouragement to a friend, a helping hand to someone struggling, can ripple through lives, communities, and even generations.

Your voice matters. Your choices matter. Your presence matters. You are part of a chain of ordinary people whose faith, actions, and love have quietly moved the world forward. Each of us is responsible for using what we have, no matter how limited it may seem, to bring light where there is darkness, hope where there is despair, and love where there is brokenness. Even in small ways, the courage to act transforms ordinary lives into extraordinary legacies. Remember the stories you've read in these pages: the mother who planted flowers in her yard after unimaginable loss, creating a vibrant path of hope for her neighbourhood; the nurse in a refugee camp who, despite exhaustion and despair, continued caring for those in need, touching lives that she would never fully know; the elderly man in

South Korea who planted trees for future generations, leaving a living gift that will endure far beyond his lifetime. These people are not extraordinary because they were perfect. They are extraordinary because they chose to act, to share their light, and to keep moving forward, even when the road was long and the outcome uncertain. You, too, can do the same.

Let this reflection serve as your personal call to action. Let it remind you that hope is a choice we must make daily, courage is a habit we must nurture, and love is a responsibility we must embrace fully. Do not wait for permission. Do not wait for the perfect moment. Begin where you are. Shine the light you have. Plant the seeds you can. Speak the words that need to be said. Offer the acts of kindness that can heal, inspire, and guide others.

Most importantly, know this: your life, story, and actions matter more than you ever realise. The moment you decide to carry your light forward, you join a movement greater than yourself—a movement that heals, inspires, and transforms lives. You become part of a legacy that will ripple through generations, offering hope to someone who needs it most.

So, rise. Step into your purpose. Let your faith become action, your hope the guiding flame, and your love the force that transforms the world. The light you carry is needed now more than ever. Share it freely, boldly, and relentlessly. Your journey is the beginning of someone else's hope, and together, our lights, each one shining uniquely, can brighten even the darkest corners of the world. Take courage. Begin today. And remember, every small spark you carry can change the world, one life at a time.

Ambassador, Dr David Rex Orgen

Dr David Rex Orgen is a best-selling author, internationally respected mental health expert, and a passionate advocate for education, cultural exchange, and community empowerment. His work spans continents, addressing critical issues such as ADHD education, boy-child advocacy, and mental health awareness in schools, workplaces, and sports. He is the UNAA Ambassador and International Coordinator for the African Continent, leading initiatives that foster unity, development, and global partnerships. Dr Orgen is also the Brand Ambassador for Livraria Lello Bookshop in Portugal, promoting literacy, arts, and the preservation of cultural heritage. As the Founder and President of InspireMind Global, Dr Orgen drives programs that uplift communities across Africa, Europe, Asia, and the United States. His leadership blends compassion with strategic action, making him a sought-after speaker, thought leader, and global change agent. With a reputation for bridging cultures and inspiring hope, Dr Orgen's mission is clear—to empower minds, transform lives, and leave a lasting legacy of wellness and education for future generations.

Conclusion

Time is a relentless river—wide, winding, and wild—carving through the landscape of history with an unyielding current. In this river, books are boats: some as fragile as paper lanterns, others as sturdy as ancient oak ships. Many volumes, though richly penned, are swept away by the surging tide—forgotten like whispers in a storm. Yet Beacon of Hope: A Catalyst for Change sails on, its hull forged in truth and its sail stitched with the golden thread of purpose. Like a lighthouse carved into the cliffs of legacy, it endures tempests of indifference and fogs of forgetfulness, shining a steady light for generations to follow. This book does not merely float; it navigates with intention—anchored in compassion, steered by vision, and destined to bless the shores of the future.

The Sound of Freedom, the Call to Hope. As this chapter of our journey together comes to a close, I am reminded of another profound moment that stirred my soul, one that perfectly encapsulates the spirit of Beacon of Hope. During one of my many visits to America, I travelled to Philadelphia in 2023, the birthplace of liberty, where I stood before the famed Liberty Bell. Cracked yet unbroken, silent yet thunderous, the bell stands as an enduring symbol of freedom, resilience, and the unrelenting spirit of humanity's quest for dignity and justice.

Liberty Bell Museum, Philadelphia

Inscribed upon it are the words from the Book of Leviticus: *"Proclaim LIBERTY Throughout all the Land unto all the Inhabitants Thereof."* As I stood in its presence, I was deeply moved. The bell's imperfection, its great crack, made it even more powerful. It was not pristine or flawless. Yet, despite its wound, it rang out for freedom across a fledgling nation, and its message still echoes today. It reminded me that hope often rises not from perfection, but perseverance. That our scars do not silence us —but rather amplify our purpose. Our broken places can become where our greatest songs are sung. The Liberty Bell called a nation to awaken.

Today, the world again needs awakening. And that call belongs to us. You, dear reader, are called a bell of liberty in your own right, to ring loud with hope, even if life has left its cracks upon you. To stand as a symbol that says: *freedom, justice, compassion, and courage are worth fighting for.* The world does not need perfect people. It needs resilient souls who are willing to shine through the cracks. It needs *Beacons of Hope*.

I urge you to carry this light forward as you return from these pages to your life. Let your voice resound like the Liberty Bell, unwavering, courageous, and full of the promise that better days are not only possible but inevitable when we dare to believe and act.

- You are the hope.
- You are the change.
- You are the legacy in motion.
- Keep ringing.
- Keep rising.
- Keep being the *Beacon of Hope* the world desperately needs now more than ever.

However, when the heart yearns to believe, the intellect will not allow it. There comes a moment, quiet and raw, when the heart whispers, maybe it's true, maybe it can happen. Possibly healing is achievable. Perhaps love will not leave this time.

Maybe the storm ***will*** pass. But just as hope dares to rise, the mind intervenes, stern and rational. *"No,"* it says. *"You have seen too much. You have been let down before. Do not build castles in the air. Protect yourself. Expect the worst."* Stuck there, between heart and head, we find ourselves torn. The heart is tender, willing to believe in miracles, holding the embers of trust. The mind? It's armoured by logic, by experience, by the bruises of battles past. This inner war is not weakness but the weight of being human. But oh, how brave it is to believe anyway. To let the heart speak louder, even if just for a moment. To give faith a voice when fear has long held the mic. To say: ***"Even if I'm wrong, I choose to hope."*** Sometimes, belief is not about proof; it's about courage.

You will always have a choice, so take courage to choose wisely. In life, we are not all dealt the same hand. Some are handed a royal flush—privilege, opportunity, support. Others receive a mismatched set—trauma, loss, struggle. However, life is not about the cards you are given. It is about how you play them. Imagine two artists. One has a full palette of vibrant colours, the other, only shades of grey. Yet the one with limited tones often creates the most moving masterpiece—blending, layering, and experimenting until beauty emerges from scarcity.

Or think of a chef with only a few simple ingredients: no lavish spices or imported delicacies. Yet with creativity and heart, they craft a dish that leaves a lasting impression because it is not about what you have but *what you make of it.*

Life is the same. Some build empires from broken pieces. Others turn pain into poetry, setbacks into steppingstones. What matters is not the hand you are dealt, but the resilience, resourcefulness, and faith with which you play it. You cannot always choose your cards, but you can choose your strategy. And that makes all the difference. Choose to be a BEACON of HOPE despite your circumstances!

Your words are seeds. Choose them wisely. Words are not just sounds or scribbles on a page. They are seeds. Whenever you speak, you plant something into someone's heart, mind, or soul. Some words bloom into wildflowers of courage and comfort. Others fester like weeds, choking joy and self-worth before it has a chance to grow. Words can be a warm coat on a winter's day or an unexpected slap in the cold. A kind sentence can build a bridge where silence once stood. A cruel one can burn down what took years to build. Think of your words like water. Are they nourishing the dry ground of someone's hope? Or are they flooding their peace with fear, shame, or doubt? You never know what someone is carrying.

But you do know what you are releasing. Your words can be a balm in a world already broken by brokenness. So, ask yourself:

- Are you a lighthouse or a lightning bolt?
- Are you lifting or wounding with the weight of your voice?
- Are you building someone's tomorrow or breaking their today?

You do not have to be perfect. But you can be intentional. Speak life. Speak love. Speak lightly. Because your words may be invisible, but their impact is not.

The best math you can learn is not taught in schools. The best math you can learn is not buried in a textbook or scribbled on a chalkboard. It is the kind that helps you *predict the future* not with tarot cards or crystal balls, but with choices, patterns, and consequences. Think of life like planting a garden. Every decision you make is a seed. Some are sunflowers, quick to bloom, but fleeting. Others are oaks that grow slowly but will provide shade for generations. Learning to *calculate future outcomes* means understanding what kind of seed you are planting today, and what kind of harvest you will get *tomorrow*.

Will that late-night Netflix binge cost you clarity in tomorrow's meeting? Will the $5 you invest daily in your skills blossom into a six-figure opportunity next year? It is compound interest, but not just for money. It is compound interest on *habits, relationships, health,* and *time*. Imagine you are steering a ship across the ocean. A one-degree turn seems tiny now, but over 1,000 miles. You will end up in a totally different country. That is how your everyday choices work. Small now, massive later. The best math is not about solving for *x*. It is about solving for *impact*. Ask yourself each day:

- If I continue this pattern, where will I end up?
- This is the math of maturity.
- That is the formula for freedom.

Turning knowledge into wisdom: the alchemy of experience. Knowledge is like gathering firewood. You can stack books, facts, and theories high, logs upon logs of potential. But until you strike a match, you do not have warmth. You do not have fire. You do not have wisdom. Wisdom happens when you *use* the knowledge—when you light it, sit beside it, and let it shape you. Think of knowledge as recipes in a cookbook. You can memorise every page and know the measurements by heart, but you will never truly understand the dish unless you step into the kitchen, get your hands messy, taste, burn, adjust, and try again. Wisdom is what lingers on your tongue after you have lived the lesson.

- Knowledge is information.
- Wisdom is transformation.

It is like knowing the directions to the mountaintop versus *climbing the mountain*. Knowledge tells you the path. Wisdom is what your legs learn with each step, your lungs learn at every altitude, and what your soul whispers when you reach the summit. Anyone can quote the truth. But wisdom knows *when* to speak it, *how* to apply it, and *why* silence sometimes speaks louder. So do not just collect knowledge like souvenirs on a shelf. Live it. Wrestle with it. Let it humble you and shape you. Only then does knowledge become richer—Wisdom is the fire that warms you and lights the way for others.

Excellence is not perfection; it is progress with purpose. Perfection is the mirage that keeps many of us crawling in the desert, parched and exhausted—never quite reaching the oasis. But excellence? Excellence is the well-tended garden that grows through seasons of trial, wind, and rain. A concert pianist may hit a wrong note in a flawless symphony, but we do not walk away saying, *"It was not excellent."* We say, *"That moved me."* Excellence lives in the *movement*, not the mistake.

Think of a diamond, beautiful, brilliant, valuable. But under the microscope, even the finest diamonds have inclusions, tiny imperfections formed under pressure. And yet, those diamonds shine the brightest. Not because they are flawless, but because they endured the fire and emerged with character. You do not need to be perfect to show up with excellence.

You just need to:

- Be intentional.
- Be consistent.
- Be willing to grow.

The Japanese art of *kintsugi* repairs broken pottery with gold, making the cracks the most beautiful part of the whole. That is excellence: embracing your journey, flaws and all, and turning your scars into strength. So today, let go of the myth of perfection. Aim for *excellence that breathes, bends, and becomes*. Because your best, given honestly and wholeheartedly, is enough.

Be the lighthouse in the storm! In January 2025, my world was rocked by three words no one wants to hear: *"You have cancer."* It was as if life had pulled the emergency brake on a speeding train. Everything halted. Everything changed. But I refused to let that diagnosis become my final destination. Instead, I saw it as a detour. It is painful, but not purposeless. I had to dig deeper than ever before. I was not just the CEO and founder of *Beacon of Hope Mission*; I became the embodiment of that beacon. Through every scan, every treatment, every lonely hospital room, I kept the light on not just for myself, but for others watching, waiting, and wondering if hope was still possible in the dark.

I am now in remission, but even more than that, I am resurrected in purpose. I documented my cancer journey so others would not have to navigate their own in silence. I turned pain into pages. I took fear and shaped it into fuel. And in 2026, I will release *Conquering Cancer Courageously*, a companion to this work, a battle cry in book form, a map for anyone walking the road I once stumbled through.

Every setback, even the ones that nearly take you out, can become the soil for a powerful comeback. Think of a seed. It breaks open in the darkness of the earth before it rises toward the sun. My journey taught me this: darkness does not cancel destiny. It *cultivates* it. **I am not the same woman who began this journey. I am not just a survivor. I am a catalyst for positive, sustainable, soul-shifting change.**

So, to you, dear reader: if you are standing in your own fire, wondering if anything good can come from the ashes, I see you. I was you. And I urge you to lift your eyes beyond the smoke. Be *big enough to HOPE beyond your daunting horizon*. Not because life is easy. But because light is powerful. And you, yes, you, were born to shine through the storm.

- Be a beacon even when hope seems bleak.
- Hope still lives regardless of circumstances; it requires cultivation.
- Aspire to be a catalyst for change.

Planting Trees You Will Never Sit Under

Legacy is not just about leaving behind something when you are gone. It is about **planting seeds in a garden you may never see bloom**. Think of your life like a quill dipped in eternal ink, with every action writing a line in your chapter and the chapters of future generations. Every kind word, courageous act, and truth you speak is a brushstroke on the mural of time. Creating a legacy is not about carving your name into stone. It is about **etching your love, wisdom, and values into the hearts of others**, like rainwater that seeps into roots, long after the storm has passed. A true legacy is a **cathedral you build, knowing you will never see the final stained glass installed**, yet you lay every stone with vision, purpose, and faith that others will take up the work and continue.

Ask yourself:

- Are you building monuments to ego or bridges of impact?
- Are you chasing applause today, or planting oaks of hope for tomorrow?
- Will your story end with your footsteps or echo in the footsteps of those you have inspired?

Legacy is not about being remembered. It is about improving the world so profoundly that forgetting you becomes impossible. Keep sowing. Keep building. Keep becoming. **Natural selection is not just for the wild; it also happens in the soul spaces**. When you show the universe who you are, time and time again, it listens. It watches. And eventually it responds. It is like standing before a blank canvas. Each choice is a bold, hesitant, vibrant, or muted brushstroke. If you refuse to paint at all, that too becomes a message. Silence speaks. Inaction echoes. People begin to interpret your canvas, not just by what you display, but by what you withhold. Are you painting a picture of courage or fear? Consistency or confusion? Integrity or illusion? The universe aligns with the art you reveal.

So be intentional with your strokes. Natural selection does not always look like survival of the fittest. Sometimes, attention drifts toward those who dare to create something honest, raw, and real.

Motivation is the spark, the sudden flash of lightning that lights up the path ahead and fills you with the energy to begin. But sparks fade. What turns that flicker into a lasting flame is execution. Execution is the daily firewood—the steady hands chopping, stacking, and feeding the fire long after the thrill of the spark is gone. Think of motivation as the wind that lifts your kite, but the string—the discipline, the daily decisions, the follow-through—keeps it soaring. Ideas may open the door, but execution builds the house, brick by brick. And those bricks become a legacy over time, something real, grounded, and lasting.

The system of life often trains people to follow the path, not to question where it leads. From a young age, we are handed blueprints: go to school, get a job, follow the rules, retire quietly. It's like being given a painted canvas and told it's a masterpiece; just stay inside the lines. But true innovation, freedom, and purpose rarely live inside the lines. They are found when you dare to paint beyond the borders, to colour the sky purple, or to scribble your own truth on a blank page. The system is smooth, predictable, and programmed like a conveyor belt. If you are not careful, it lulls you into motion without meaning. But stepping off that belt takes courage. It's choosing to build your own road when everyone else is queuing for the same bus. So, think strategically. Question the norm. Create effectively. Life is not meant to be copied; it's meant to be *crafted*.

Excuses are like treadmills; you are moving but going nowhere

They may make you feel like you are doing something, but you are still stuck in the same spot, just a little more tired. Excuses are the fog that clouds the mirror, making it easier to blur the truth—but the reflection does not lie. Results, on the other hand, are bricks. Every action and step lays one more stone in the foundation of your legacy. You cannot build a house with excuses, but you can build an empire with effort. Think of your dreams like seeds. Excuses are the weeds that choke them, while results are the sunlight and water they crave. One drains, the other grows. Make the sage decision today to trade your "someday" for "today," your "can't" for "how." In the end, excuses will fade, but the results will speak for a long time after you have moved on. And HOPE will always prevail, so craft it intentionally.

Kelly Markey
km
CEO: Markey Writing Academy
Founder: Beacon of Hope Mission
Global Award Winning Publisher
International Bestselling & Award Winning Author
Brand Ambassador: Global Movement of Hope
Featured on New York Times Square Billboard
kellymarkey.com

Kelly Markey

- CEO of Markey Writing Academy (Global Publishing House).
- Founder and Global Director of Beacon of Hope Mission.
- Kelly Markey is a five-time international bestselling and award-winning author.
- Finalist for the Woman Changing the World award in London.
- Winner of the top executive award (IAOTP, New York).
- Brand Ambassador for the global movement of hope in Canada.
- Winner of the top book of the year in New York for "The Life of Jayandra" (2024)
- Nominated by KWE for the Kingdom Culture Award in Australia.
- MWA publication, "Echoes of humanity," FINALIST for book of the year in Australia.
- In New York, the Beacon of Hope Mission board awarded Kelly Markey the Diamond Excellence Award for being a global catalyst for hope and change.
- Nominated by Lifeline for the Queen book award in South Africa
- Global philanthropist, one of her long-term partnerships is with Lifeline: Zululand in South Africa and the Cancer Council in Australia.

- Featured on the New York Times Square Billboard.
- Australian Christian Business Award, Winner, 2025
- Christian Women Entrepreneurs Network of Africa, Finalist, 2025
- Cancer Survivor and Advocate
- Suicide Awareness Architect

Kelly is a passionate advocate for social justice, human rights, and equality. She works tirelessly to raise awareness about suicide, integrity, and discrimination, and brings HOPE to humanity. Kelly has been featured on numerous radio stations, newspapers, podcasts, multiple television channels, and numerous cover features of magazines worldwide. She speaks five different languages and is an avid traveller. She has a cosmopolitan global network. Kelly Markey holds the hearts and minds of die-hard bookworms all around the world. Kelly is a captivating wordsmith born in the fiery year of the Tiger. Hailing from a small town with big dreams, Markey's journey as an author is as bold and adventurous as the symbol that defines her birth year.

Awards

BEACON OF HOPE
KELLY MARKEY

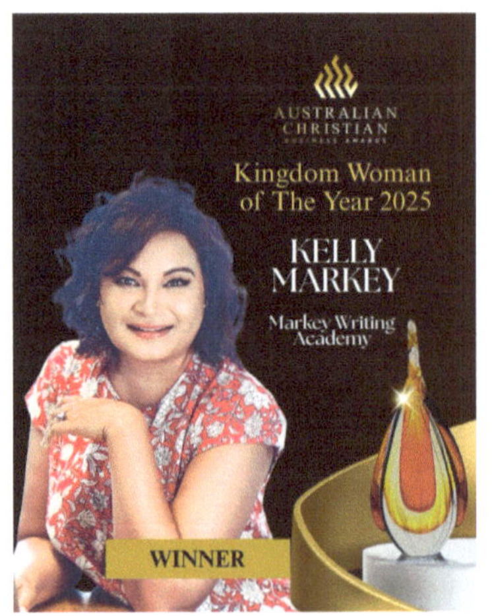
AUSTRALIAN
CHRISTIAN
Kingdom Woman
of The Year 2025
KELLY
MARKEY
Markey Writing
Academy
WINNER

Markey Writing Academy

Kelly is the Founder and CEO of Markey Writing Academy, her global publishing house that has helped others achieve their dreams of becoming successful international authors.

Welcome to Markey Writing Academy, where words transform into art and stories ignite minds.

At Markey Writing Academy, we are not just a publishing company but are passionate about nurturing talent and crafting exceptional narratives that captivate readers worldwide. Whether you are an aspiring author with a manuscript seeking publication or a seasoned writer looking to refine your craft, our academy offers a tailored approach to meet your literary aspirations.

What sets us apart? Our commitment to personalised guidance, unparalleled editorial support, and a keen understanding of the evolving publishing landscape. We believe in empowering writers with the knowledge and tools to succeed in today's competitive market. From manuscript evaluation to strategic marketing advice, our team of industry experts carefully curates every step of your publishing journey.

Join Markey Writing Academy and embark on a transformative experience where your words gain resonance, and your stories find their audience. Let your journey to literary excellence begin with us.

Visit us at Markey Writing Academy and discover why your story deserves our dedication. www.kellymarkey.com

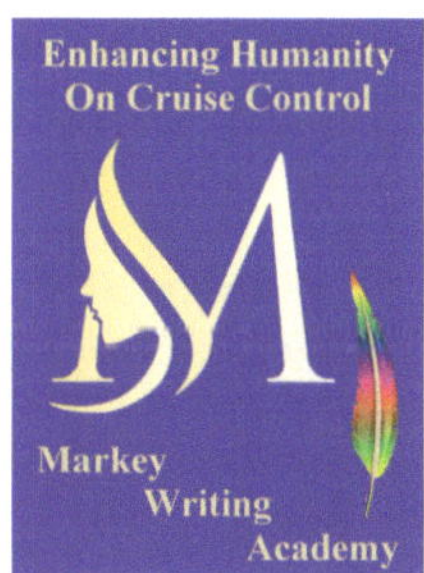

Beacon of Hope Mission

Kelly Markey is the Founder and CEO of Beacon of Hope and Social Change Mission, a non-profit social enterprise. We invest our profit into the global community. At Beacon of Hope, we are dedicated to uplifting narratives and empowering voices to inspire positive social change. We believe in the transformative power of stories to foster empathy, understanding, and action.

What We Stand For

Inspiring Change: We ignite conversations that inspire transformation and unity, challenge perspectives, and shed light on the human experience.

Promoting Suicide Prevention: We are committed to raising awareness and promoting initiatives that support wellbeing and prevent suicide.

Advocating for Mental Health: Through our publications, we champion mental health awareness and provide a platform for voices that encourage understanding and compassion.

Championing Social Change: Our collection of literature serves as a platform for underrepresented communities, highlighting issues that demand societal attention and advocating for justice and inclusivity.

Enhancing Longevity: Promoting holistic living and proactive choices, especially for cancer patients.

Enhancing Literacy: We create awareness about reading and the doors it will open. We ignite the spark of HOPE that literacy, education, and inspiration will unlock brighter futures.

Why We Do It

Guided by Kelly Markey's vision and dedication, our mission transcends mere publication. We aim to make a tangible difference in the world by fostering empathy, advocating for justice, and striving for a more inclusive society. Each title we publish embodies the ethos of social change, offering readers a glimpse into lives, struggles, and triumphs they might not otherwise encounter.

Join Me

We invite you to join us in our mission to empower communities and individuals. Together, we can embrace empathy, advocate for justice, and inspire change through the power of storytelling.

Sponsorship

Visit my website to sponsor our strategic goals.

Beacon of Hope Mission Forum

In an increasingly interconnected world, the need for hope and positive action has never been more critical. The annual International Beacon of Hope Forum is a vital platform to foster awareness, share experiences, and ignite change across borders. This forum is essential in our collective journey toward a brighter future.

A Global Gathering for Change

The Beacon of Hope Forum brings together individuals, organisations, and thought leaders from diverse backgrounds. This confluence of perspectives allows for rich dialogue on the challenges facing different communities. By highlighting local issues and global trends, participants can learn from one another and develop strategies that resonate across cultures.

Raising Awareness About Hope Initiatives

At the heart of the forum is a commitment to promoting hope-driven initiatives. By showcasing successful projects and innovative solutions, the forum helps to inspire others to act in their communities. This exchange of ideas is crucial for fostering a culture of hope transcending geographic boundaries.

Empowering Voices and Sharing Stories

Every participant at the forum has a unique story to tell. By providing a platform for these narratives, we amplify the voices of those often unheard. Sharing personal experiences humanises the issues we face and builds empathy and solidarity among attendees. This connection is essential for cultivating a global community dedicated to making a difference.

Fostering Collaboration and Partnerships

The forum is more than just a series of talks; it's a launchpad for collaboration. By facilitating partnerships between organisations, businesses, and governments, we can leverage resources and expertise to tackle pressing challenges. The collective power of united efforts can lead to impactful, scalable solutions that bring hope to even the most vulnerable communities.

Highlighting the Role of Education and Awareness

Education is a cornerstone of empowerment. The forum emphasises spreading knowledge about critical issues, from suicide prevention to social justice. By educating participants and the broader public, we can cultivate informed advocates equipped to inspire change in their communities.

Inspiring Action and Commitment

The goal of the Beacon of Hope Forum is to inspire action. Whether through advocacy, volunteering, or donating, participants leave with a renewed sense of purpose. We can transform hope into tangible outcomes by fostering a sense of accountability and commitment.

www.beaconofhopemission.com

Beacon of Hope Awards

The International Beacon of Hope Forum is not just an event; it's a movement. By gathering diverse voices and fostering collaboration, we aim to illuminate pathways of hope worldwide. As we share stories, inspire action, and build connections, we take vital steps toward creating a future where hope thrives in every corner of the globe. Together, we can turn awareness into action and dreams into reality.

The Beacon of Hope Committee honours people from around the world who are proactive in being a beacon of hope to the world with a Beacon of Hope Award.

Michelle Jewlal: Beacon of Hope Award for Strategic Business Discretion

Loschinee Naiker: Beacon of Hope Award for Community Stewardship with Distinction

Faye Marks: Beacon of Hope Award for Poetic Justice and Mental Health Awareness Excellence

www.beaconofhopemission.com

Top Book of the Year

In this poignant narrative that delves into the profound journey of Jayandra, a soul grapples with the complexities of existence and the resolute determination to find meaning.

Through eloquent prose and heartfelt introspection, the author, Kelly Markey, masterfully weaves together themes of resilience, hope, and the human spirit's indomitable will.

Recognised for its profound impact and literary brilliance, *"The Life of Jayandra"* has captured hearts worldwide, earning the prestigious title of Top Book of the Year 2024 – IAOTP.

Now, witness its powerful message illuminated on the iconic New York Times Square Billboard, a testament to its enduring significance and universal acclaim that mandates change. Join Kelly Markey on a transformative odyssey that transcends boundaries and resonates deeply with readers everywhere. Embrace a narrative that not only compels us to introspect on the suicide landscape but also enlightens and invites us to ponder life's profound questions and celebrate the triumph of the human spirit.

An exceptional tribute to Jayandra, gone too soon, but leaving a PROFOUND LEGACY.

Featured on the New York Times Square Billboard

I prefer to have my brother here rather than this book. Yet this is the reality, and this book has begun the great work for reform on the taboo topic of suicide.

Being featured on the New York Times Square Billboard is no small feat. WOW, thank you, God. Romans 8:28, *"And we know that all things work together for good."*

Jayandra, your absence gets louder and longer, my sweet brother, but something profound prevails in the void.

I am grateful for the incredible support and enthusiasm as I was featured on the New York Times Square Billboard. It was a once-in-a-lifetime milestone, and sharing that moment with others, whether in person or online, made it even more special.

Whether cheering me on in New York or tuning in from afar, your encouragement and presence meant more to me than words can express. Thank you for being a part of this epic experience and making it a memory I will cherish forever with heartfelt thanks.

Acknowledgements

Beacon of Hope: Catalyst for Change was born not from ease, but from resilience, community, and the unwavering belief that light can pierce even the darkest moments. I am deeply grateful to the global network of co-authors whose dedication to collective progress and grassroots transformation continues to inspire the heartbeat of this book. Your work uplifts lives and lights the path for others—thank you for being true catalysts of change.

Sincere appreciation to Julienne Ryan for penning a heartfelt foreword and continued support despite international borders. I am incredibly grateful to all the global media outlets that reviewed this book.

To my readers worldwide, thank you for welcoming our words into your lives and hearts. Your continued support, encouragement, and messages of hope are why this mission lives on. If this book has stirred something within you, I humbly invite you to leave a review on **Goodreads**. Your voice helps this message travel even further.

To my extraordinary editor, thank you for sharpening our words without dulling their soul.

And to the dedicated team at **Markey Writing Academy**, your belief in the power of storytelling continues to create ripples across the globe.

In addition, I am especially thankful to those who stood behind the curtain, offering strength and encouragement during one of the most trying seasons of my life—navigating cancer while still showing up, writing, and believing in tomorrow. You reminded me that even in silence, support can speak volumes.

Your life is a candle; whether it flickers in a palace or a prison, it still holds the power to light the way.

Leadership is not about titles or perfect conditions. It is about showing up like a lighthouse in the storm—steady, even when the wind howls. You may not choose your circumstances, but you *do* choose your response. And in a world dimmed by doubt, your integrity, kindness, and courage can be the match that sets others ablaze with hope. Leading by example is like planting seeds in dry soil. You may not see the bloom today, but someone, someday, will eat fruit from the tree you chose to nurture. Even on the hardest days, your consistency becomes someone else's compass.

Remember, we all have a limited number of sunsets. Use yours to cast long shadows of goodness, impact, and truth. Make your impact. Thank you, and I acknowledge you for all you have done and will do.

This book is not just mine; it belongs to everyone who chooses to hope, heal, and rise.

kellymarkey.com

beaconofhopemission.com

www.ingramcontent.com/pod-product-compliance
Lightning Source LLC
Chambersburg PA
CBHW042035180726
48295CB00006B/102

9781763683754